This book belongs to

Name .Christina .Brynes...............

Address ....

.................................,......................

Company ....

....

Date of first meeting ....

the guide handbook

the guide handbook

© The Girl Guides Association 1992
First published 1992
Reprinted 1992 (twice), 1993

ISBN 0 85260 111 5

Typeset by
CRB Typesetting Services
Ely, Cambs.
Colour repro by
Godfrey Lang Ltd, London
Paper supplied by
Precision Publishing Papers, Yeovil
Printed in Great Britain by
Bath Press Colourbooks, Glasgow

The Girl Guide Handbook is printed on paper produced by
Biberist, an environmentally friendly paper mill,
meeting Swiss emission control standards, which are the most
stringent in the world. The paper is totally chlorine free.

the
guide
handbook

Published by
The Girl Guides Association
17–19 Buckingham Palace Road,
London SW1W 0PT

Guiders are reminded that during the life span of this publication, policy changes may be made by the GGA which will affect the accuracy of information contained within these pages.

the guide handbook

Editorial:
Charlotte Evans, Gillian Sutton and Ann Moynihan

Design:
Angie Foster and Anne Moffat

Illustrations:
Caroline Smith; front cover, chapters 1, 3, 5, 7, 9 and PS
Cheryl Tarbuck; chapters 6, 8 and 10
Alison Wisenfeld; chapters 2 and 4

Acknowledgements

Members of the working group: Annaliese Barrall, Kath Bill,
Linda Blatchford, Eryl Evans, Joan Hazell, Carol Horne,
Jane Lewes, Ann Mitchell, Jenny Read,
Ruth Sara, Jane Thompson.

Girl Guides Association Advisers: Sheila Edwards, Judy Ellis,
Pauline McKie, Sheila Mountford, Carol Selwyn-Jones,
Doreen Sporle and Sue Taylor.

and a special thanks to all the Guides and Guiders who read
and wrote drafts of the Handbook.

©The electronic plant-watering device instructions on pages
152-153 are reproduced from *The Usborne Book of Science
Fun* by permission of Usborne Publishing Ltd, London.

The GGA wish to thank Ordnance Survey for kind permission
to reproduce the maps between pages 66 and 73.

CONTENTS

1

welcome to guides

Welcome! You're about to become part of the

biggest Movement there has ever been for

young people like you.

There are millions of Guides all over the

world, hundreds of thousands in the

United Kingdom, thousands in your county, maybe a

hundred or more in your

District, lots in your

Company, six or more in

your Patrol . . . and now you!

This book won't tell you all about being a Guide, but it will help you with lots of ideas, get you thinking and help you record what you do.

It will tell you some of the things you need to know about before you become a Guide, and will help you decide what you want to do when you are a Guide.

One thing you will have to do before you become a Guide is a set of Pre-Promise Challenges which will help you make friends with other Guides and get to know some of the things they do.

WHAT DO GIRL GUIDES DO?

As a Guide you will ...

go places

make things happen

try new things

learn to look after yourself

be part of a small group of friends

think about your faith and how to live your life

help to change the world

be part of something which is worldwide

work with people

If you want to know more about:
- **Guides** go to page 11
- **your Patrol and Company** go to page 9
- **the Guide family** go to page 8
- **the Pre-Promise Challenges** go to page 14

welcome to guides

7

THE GUIDE FAMILY IN THE UK

There are many parts of the Guide family. How many do you already know?

Every member wears a uniform to show she is a Guide. You can choose any clothes from the Guide uniform collection and wear them for any occasion, as long as they are safe and comfortable and you are happy to wear them.

Look after your uniform and wear it with pride – it shows you are a member of a worldwide Movement helping to make the world a better place.

·BROWNIE GUIDES·

·GUIDES·

·RANGERS·

Other people involved in Guiding are: Lone Guides and Rangers, Supporters – like Friends of Guiding, LINK and the Trefoil Guild

·YOUNG LEADERS·

·RAINBOW GUIDES·

·GUIDERS·

YOUR UNIT

A group of lions is called a pride, a collection of flamingoes is called a flock and a number of Patrols who regularly meet together is called a **unit** or a **Company**.

Your regular Guide meetings will usually be for the whole unit. Part of the meeting should be Patrol time – a chance for each Patrol to get together to do things on its own. Sometimes you might all go out together somewhere instead of using your normal meeting place – and for a lot of Guides, one of the highlights of the year is a camp or holiday away from home.

The unit is run by the Patrol Leaders' Council (known as the PLC), helped by the Guiders. The Patrol Leaders find out from the Guides in their Patrols what they would like to do and take all the ideas to a meeting of the Patrol Leaders' Council, where they work out a programme of activities for the unit to do during the next few weeks.

There are meetings of the Patrol Leaders' Council as often as they are needed, but usually at least once a term.

As well as deciding on the unit's programme, the PLC has other jobs. Some of the things the Patrol Leaders' Council might decide are:

- **where** to go to camp;
- **whether** the unit should wear neckerchiefs or not;
- **how much** your subscription should be and when it should be paid (every week, once a term etc);
- **whether** to buy a new tent or a cassette recorder (or how to raise enough money for both!);
- **what activities** the whole unit will do together.

The adults who look after the Company are called **Guiders**; they don't run everything, but they do guide the Guides!

For more information about:
- Patrols   see page 24
- camping   see page 98
- the PLC   see page 28

FIND OUT ABOUT YOUR PATROL

Our Patrol's name is

_____

Our Patrol Leader is

_____

Our Patrol Second is

_____

Our Patrol
emblem is

Ask each member of your Patrol to sign her name here:

_____

_____

_____

_____

_____

Our Patrol contact is

_____

(Let her know if you have to miss a meeting)

tel _____

welcome to guides

Fill in these details about your Company:

Name _____

Names of Patrols _____

_____

We meet on _____ **from** _____

to _____ **at** _____

Our Company is part of _____ **District**

My Guider's name is _____

Address _____

_____ **tel** _____

Assistant Guider _____

Address _____

_____ **tel** _____

Assistant Guider _____

Address _____

_____ **tel** _____

Unit Helper _____

Address _____

_____ **tel** _____

Young Leader _____

Address _____

_____ **tel** _____

YOUR PATROL

It's always a good feeling to have someone to talk to, to share things with, to help and who will help you. That's why in Guides we have Patrols.

A Patrol is a small group of friends who are Guides, or Guides who are friends.

We have badgers in our village so we're Badger Patrol

All our Patrols are named after famous women – we're Astor Patrol

You will do most of the things you do in Guides in your Patrol. A Patrol is just the right size – small enough so that everyone feels welcome and needed, large enough to be a real team!

HOW GUIDES GOT THEIR NAME

Robert Baden-Powell was a famous soldier who fought in the Boer War in South Africa at the beginning of the 20th century. During the Siege of Mafeking, when the town and the British soldiers were besieged by Boer soldiers, B-P noticed how the young boys made themselves useful by carrying messages for the soldiers. When he came home, he decided to put some of his 'scouting' ideas into practice to see if they would be any good for young boys and he took 21 boys camping on Brownsea Island, near Poole in Dorset. The camp was a great success, and B-P wrote his book *Scouting for Boys*, full of exciting things for boys to do like tracking, signalling and cooking. Soon boys began to organize themselves into Patrols and Troops and called themselves 'Boy Scouts'.

However, lots of girls bought the book as well and, even though it was much more difficult for girls in those days to get out and about, they too formed themselves into Patrols of Girl Scouts and did all the things the boys did. By 1909

over 6,000 girls had registered at Scout Headquarters (using only their initials so that no one would spot they were girls!).

In 1909 there was a Boy Scout Rally at Crystal Palace in London. Among all the thousands of Boy Scouts there was also a group of girls, who spoke to B-P and asked him to

let girls be Scouts. B-P decided that he would have to do something for the girls.

In those days, girls led very narrow lives and the idea of them going camping and hiking wasn't very popular with a lot of people as this extract from the Scout newspaper shows:

'If a girl is not allowed to run, or even hurry, to swim, ride a bike, or raise her arms above her head, how can she become a Scout?'
SCOUT HEADQUARTERS GAZETTE 1909.

B-P knew that if he called the girls Scouts, not only would the boys be annoyed that girls were joining in, but parents would be unhappy about their daughters becoming tomboys and mixing with boys. His career had been in the British army.

One of the many regiments he had served with was a famous Indian regiment called the Khyber Guides, who served on the north-west frontier of India. They were famous because they were trained to do almost anything, worked hard, could look after themselves and had lots of common sense. B-P persuaded the girl 'Scouts' that Guides was a very special name of which they could be proud. So …

In 1910 the first Girl Guides began!

● There are several books you can read to find out about the history of Guiding. Ask your Guider if you can have a copy of *1910 … and Then?* or a biography of B-P.

THE WORLDWIDE GUIDE FAMILY

Since 1910 Guides have spread very rapidly and there are now about eight million Guides in countries all over the world. The World Association of Girl Guides and Girl Scouts (WAGGGS) was formed to link together Guides all over the world. In some countries the girls preferred to call themselves 'Girl Scouts'.

ALL GIRL GUIDES AND GIRL SCOUTS SHARE:

● **The Guide Promise** – each country has its own Promise but all have the same three parts: duty to God or to your religion; duty to your country; keeping the Guide Law.

● **The Good Turn** – each Guide tries to do a kind thing for someone else, without payment and without being asked, every day.

● **The World Badge** – this can be worn on your uniform or on your ordinary clothes. The three leaves of the trefoil stand for the

threefold Promise. The vein in the centre is a compass needle, pointing the way, and the two stars stand for the Promise and Law. The 'stalk' at the bottom is a heraldic 'feu' or fire, standing for the love of mankind. The colours stand for the golden sun shining over all the children of the world from a blue sky.

● **The World Flag** – this is in the same colours as the World Badge and can be carried or flown by any member of the Movement. You probably have it as your unit flag.

● **The Guide Sign** – the three fingers stand for the three parts of the Promise. You use the Guide sign when you make or renew your Promise and you can use it when you meet other Guides.

You might also use it when you receive a badge or at the end of meetings.

● **The Motto – BE PREPARED.** This means that Guides are ready to cope with anything that might come their way.

● **The Left Handshake** – this is the way members of the Movement greet each other. The left hand is the one nearest the heart and so shows friendship.

● **Thinking Day** – on the 22nd February each year Guides think of their Guide sisters all around the world. The date was chosen at a World Conference because it was the birthday of both the Founder and the World Chief Guide.

- **The World Centres** – every Guide is a home owner! You have four Guide homes in different parts of the world. They are: Our Chalet in Switzerland, Pax Lodge in London, Our Cabaña in Mexico, Sangam in India.

Our Chalet

Sangam

Pax Lodge

Our Cabaña

- **The World Chief Guide** – Olave, Lady Baden-Powell is the only person ever to have been World Chief Guide. She was the wife of the Founder, Lord Robert Baden-Powell of Gilwell and lived from 1889 to 1977.

welcome to guides

13

THE PRE-PROMISE CHALLENGE

It wouldn't be much fun if when you went to your first meeting you were handed a book and told 'Read this – it will tell you all about Guides!' No, the only way you can get to know about Guides is to be with them for a while, doing what they do and learning a little bit about why they do it.

That's why, before you really become a Guide by making the Promise, you need to find out a bit about what Guides do.

You do this by completing **eight Pre-Promise Challenges**.

WHAT IS A CHALLENGE?

Well, the dictionary says two things. One is that a challenge is 'a difficult or demanding task' and the other is that a challenge is 'an invitation to take part in something'. Challenges in Guides are a mixture of both, but are more like the second answer than the first!

When you accept a Challenge you choose something you have never done before, or something you would like to do differently. Then you work out how to do it and when. And then you do it!

WHY EIGHT?

Why not ten? or six? or a hundred? Because of this:

Guiding is fun, but it is also about getting to know the world. These eight headings or Points help us to make sure that we aren't missing anything in the world. Everything Guides do comes back to one or more of the Eight Points.

If you were a Brownie you will probably recognize these ideas – this is because everyone in Guiding follows more or less the same programme – but it grows with you.

Remember the Eight Points – you'll meet them again!

THE PRE-PROMISE CHALLENGES

Talk about what you want to do with your Patrol Leader or Guider. Tick the challenge you have chosen and ask your Patrol Leader, Guider or someone at home to sign the space below each one when you have completed it. If you like you can choose something completely different to do for your challenges – write it in the space provided.

1 ENJOYING THE OUT-OF-DOORS

☐ Join in an outdoor activity with your Patrol (such as a hike, a wide game, cooking, an act of worship, a sport)
or
☐ Learn something that would be useful out-of-doors (such as reading a bus or train timetable; using a compass; trails; weather signs)
or
☐ Learn more about something you find out-of-doors (such as trees, birds, the stars, rocks)
OR

☐ . . . .
signed . . . .

2 KEEPING FIT

☐ Show in a game or agility challenge that you are lively and energetic
or
☐ Keep a record for a week to show you can keep up a daily good-health habit (such as keeping fit, caring for your teeth, cutting down on sweets and crisps)
or
☐ Show each week at your meeting that you have taken trouble to look clean, neat and suitably dressed
OR

☐ . . . .
signed . . . .

3 THINKING FOR YOURSELF

☐ Join in a game or Patrol activity where you have to think (this could be a memory test or a puzzle to work out)
or
☐ Learn something by heart that will help you as a Guide (such as a Guide song, the Country Code, Guide signals made with hands or whistles)
or
☐ Choose which items of uniform you will wear when you are a Guide

OR

☐ . . . .
signed . . . .

4 GIVING SERVICE

☐ Join in a Patrol Good Turn or service project
or
☐ Learn something that will be useful in giving service (such as how to treat a graze, how to call the emergency services, the manual alphabet)
or
☐ Think of and carry out a personal piece of service (such as weeding a flower bed, an anti-litter campaign, visiting someone in hospital)
OR

☐ . . . .
signed . . . .

5 EXPLORING THE ARTS

☐ Make something yourself and show it to your Patrol (such as a mask, a picture frame, a photo story)
or
☐ Join with your Patrol in a play, dance, song etc
or
☐ Write a story, poem or play

and share it with your Patrol
OR

☐ . . . .

signed . . . .

6 BECOMING A HOMEMAKER

☐ Undertake a new regular job at home (such as making or changing your bed, putting the rubbish out, watering the plants, or washing the car)
or
☐ Learn how to do something which will be useful at home (such as how to cook a favourite dish, how to change a lightbulb, how to use an iron)
or
☐ Join with your Patrol in a homecraft activity
OR

☐ . . . .

signed . . . .

7 KEEPING THE GUIDE LAW

☐ Learn the Guide Law and understand what it means
or
☐ Think of something connected with one part of the Guide Law that you will undertake to do while you are preparing to be a Guide (such

as exercising someone's dog, getting up as soon as you are called, being punctual) – then carry it out!
or
☐ Take part in a Patrol activity about the Guide Law
OR

☐ . . . .

signed . . . .

8 GETTING TO KNOW PEOPLE

☐ Join in with your Patrol at a Patrol meeting or discussion
or
☐ Learn something interesting about each member of your Patrol (such as where they go to school, where they live, how many brothers or sisters they have) or about your Guiders
or
☐ Do a job for your Patrol
or
☐ Find out about B-P and the early days of Guiding
OR

☐ . . . .

signed . . . .

THE PROMISE ... AND WHAT IT MEANS TO MAKE IT

Let's look at the Promise:

**I promise that I will do my best:
To do my duty to God,
To serve the Queen and help other people, and
To keep the Guide Law.**

The Guide Promise is not a 'secret password' you say once to join and never think about again – it matters that you understand it and think about what it means for you. It's important that you feel that you can make this Promise,

because it will be at the heart of everything you do in Guiding.

Every member of this worldwide Movement has made the Promise (or one very like it) and is trying to keep it. Now it's your turn. What does it mean?

I PROMISE ...

When you say this it means that you have given your word that you are going to do what you say. If you always try to keep promises, people will know that you can be trusted.

... THAT I WILL DO MY BEST ...

Nobody's asking you to

be perfect. Your best isn't the same as anyone else's best. Only you know how hard you have tried.

... TO DO MY DUTY TO GOD ...

People belong to many different religions and express their belief in God in many different ways.

For many people it means being part of a worshipping community – a church, synagogue, mosque or temple – where they can find out about the teaching and traditions of their faith, and learn how to make their faith matter in their everyday lives.

Others don't feel as if they belong to any religion, but they do believe in God, and they try to do what they think God would like them to do.

As a Guide you agree to do your duty to God, whether you regularly go to a place of worship or not. How do you think you can do this in your own life?

● One way is to learn about the teachings of your faith
● One way is to think about what God would like you to be, and to keep trying to be like that
● One way is by looking after the world God has made

● One way is by helping and caring for the people in the world
● One way is to help others understand your faith so that they are not wary of you.

'God has made me as a human being. Not a camel, not an oak tree, not a dolphin. That means he wants me to be a human being, so I will try to be the best human being I can be.'

The Founder said: 'Religion seems a very simple thing: 1. Love and serve God 2. Love and serve your neighbour'.

O great Spirit Whose voice I hear in the winds And whose breath gives life to all the world Hear me! I am small and weak I need your strength and wisdom
Sioux

'I read in a book about a man called Jesus who went about doing good. It disconcerts me to realize that I just go about.'

Showing respect for the religious beliefs of others is an important part of Guiding. Some people's beliefs may be very different from yours. How can you show you respect the religious beliefs of others?

Start finding out about different faiths. Draw a symbol of your own faith in the first box, then discover symbols from four different faiths and draw them in the other boxes.

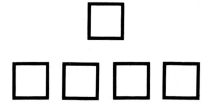

... TO SERVE THE QUEEN ...

Wherever you see the Queen, whether it's on television or, if you're very lucky, in person, she's usually doing something for other people. When you were very young you might have wanted to be a queen or a princess, because you could do what you liked all day. But if you look at the Queen's busy life you can see that it isn't like that at all. It can't be very nice to be watched everywhere you go, even on holiday!

When she was 21 the Queen promised her subjects:

'My whole life, whether it be long or short, shall be devoted to your service and the service of our great imperial family to which we all belong, but I shall not have the strength to carry out this resolution unless you join in it with me.'

She promised to serve us with our help. How can we help?
We can look after our community.
We can keep the laws of our country.
We can learn to think for ourselves, so that when we are older we can take responsibility for other people.
We can find out about our own country, its history and customs, so that we can tell other people about it.
We can be good citizens at home and abroad.

... AND HELP OTHER PEOPLE ...

If you helped someone today think about what you did. Did you do it willingly? Did it matter if no one thanked you? Could you have helped someone, but decided not to? Why? Service is an important part of Guiding.

Helping others is fun and it will make you feel good when you see how other people benefit.

See page 10 for more information about giving service.

... AND TO KEEP THE GUIDE LAW.

There are ten parts to the Guide Law.
1 A Guide is loyal and can be trusted.
2 A Guide is helpful.
3 A Guide is polite and considerate.
4 A Guide is friendly and a sister to all Guides.
5 A Guide is kind to animals and respects all living things.
6 A Guide is obedient.
7 A Guide has courage and is cheerful in all difficulties.
8 A Guide makes good use of her time.
9 A Guide takes care of her own possessions and those of other people.
10 A Guide is self-controlled in all she thinks, says and does.

Most rules are lists of things starting 'do not ...', but as you can see, all these Laws are about *doing*.

You'll find that some parts of the Law are easy to keep, and some are more difficult. But if you try your best to keep them every day they will become easier.
☐ Think of situations where Guides are forgetting or remembering the Guide Law and act or mime them out.

MAKING YOUR PROMISE

When you have completed the Promise challenges and feel ready to make your Promise then you and your Patrol can begin to plan your Promise ceremony. As long as you use the words on the next page you can make your Promise anywhere you like, whenever you like (within reason!).

IF YOU WERE A BROWNIE

Your Guider says: 'As a Brownie you have already promised to do your best to do your duty to God, to serve the Queen and help other people.

Are you willing to renew this, and to promise to do your best to keep the Guide Law?'

You say: 'Yes, I promise that I will do my best: To do my duty to God, To serve the Queen and help other people, and To keep the Guide Law.

IF YOU WERE NOT A BROWNIE

Your Guider says: 'Do you understand that as a Guide you will be trusted to do your best to do your duty to God, to serve the Queen and help other people and to keep the Guide Law?'

You say: 'Yes'

Your Guider says: 'Are you willing to make your Promise as a Guide?'

You say: 'Yes. I promise that I will do my best: To do my duty to God, To serve the Queen and help other people, and to keep the Guide Law.'

IN BOTH CASES YOUR GUIDER THEN SAYS:

'I trust you to keep this Promise and to try to do at least one Good Turn every day.' Your Guider will then pin on your badge and welcome you as a Guide.

You could make your Promise ...

**by candle light
at camp
on a night hike
at a place of worship
on an adventurous activity
at a camp fire**

I promise that I will do my best:
To do my duty to God,
To serve the Queen
And help other people,
And to keep the Guide Law.

I made my promise
on.................at.................signed.................

WHAT NOW?

Now that you are a Guide you will try all sorts of interesting and exciting activities. Many of the things you will be doing are explained later in this Handbook. Use your Handbook as a 'dip-into' book – you don't have to start at the beginning and work all the way through!

To help you plan your time in Guides there are four Trefoil Badges you can work for. These Badges help you to keep your Promise in a practical way.

The Trefoil Badges are:

Yellow	on page 205
Green	on page 206
Red	on page 207
Blue	on page 209

If you join Guides straight from Brownies you will probably start on the Yellow Trefoil, but if you are older you should talk with your Patrol Leader and your Guider about starting with one of the others. Normally you should begin with the Trefoil other girls of your age are working on, but you might want to try some of the activities from an earlier Trefoil until you get the hang of Guiding!

There is also a special award, called the Baden-Powell Award, which you can work for when you are doing your Blue Trefoil.

and Patrol Interest Pennants and the Patrol Purpose Patch to do with your Patrol.

Full details of all Guide badges, pennants and patches can be found in the Guide Badge Book.

If an activity in this handbook has a symbol like this ♣ beside it it will help you with one of the Trefoil Badges.

Other activities have a box beside them for you to tick. There are lots of Interest Badges, which you can do on your own or with your Patrol,

At the end of your first meeting, you will hear the Guides sing a special song. It's called 'Taps', and goes like this:

Day is done, Gone the sun, From the sea, from the hills, from the sky. All is well, Safe ly rest, God is nigh.

Sometimes you will sing the daytime version:

**Thanks and praise,
For our days,
'Neath the sun,
'neath the stars, 'neath the sky.
As we go,
This we know,
God is nigh.**

The word 'Taps' comes from the early days of the American army. At the end of the day, the drummer would tap on his drum so that the soldiers would know that it was time to go to bed for the night. Even when the army replaced the drum with a bugle, the name still stuck.

USING YOUR HAND-BOOK

The activities in this book will help you progress in the Eight Point Programme:

enjoying the out-of-doors

thinking for yourself

exploring the arts

keeping the Guide Law

keeping fit

giving service

becoming a homemaker

getting to know people

Often an activity will help you learn about more than one point.

2

As a Guide you will do some things with your Guider and all the Guides in your unit, and you will do some things by yourself,

but most of what you do as

✭ HIKING ✭

a Guide will be done

with your Patrol.

Many Patrols are

called after flowers and birds, but you may also be named after animals, stars, famous people or trees, almost anything else which is attractive and inspiring.

your patrol and you

WHAT IS A PATROL?

A Patrol is:

A GROUP OF FOUR TO EIGHT GIRLS ✶ A GROUP WHERE EVERYBODY IS IMPORTANT ✶

A GROUP OF FRIENDS ✶

A GROUP THAT PLANS TOGETHER AND DOES THINGS TOGETHER ✶

A GROUP THAT CHOOSES ITS OWN LEADER AND WHERE THE LEADER CHOOSES HER OWN SECOND ✶

• a Patrol corner for meeting, doing things and talking.

• Patrol equipment — useful things for Patrol and unit meetings. Just what you have depends on what your Patrol likes doing and the sort of things you do with your unit. The pictures give you some suggestions.

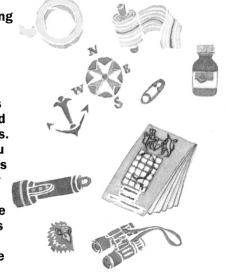

A Patrol has:
• an emblem — Patrols choose their own name and emblem. Traditionally Patrols are named after birds and flowers, but you can have any name you want. You can buy flower and bird emblems ready made from Guide shops, or blank ones on which you can sew or paint your own design.

You might also have a box of equipment for camp.

Use your Patrol emblem or colours to show things are yours. You may have a Patrol box you can keep things in at your meeting place, but if you can't leave anything there you can keep it all in a small bag or case and bring it to each meeting.

25

□ Make a Patrol log book  Have a laugh looking back on what you did as a Patrol by making a Patrol log book. Write short accounts of your Patrol and its activities. Illustrate it with drawings and photos. Stick in things that remind you of places: tickets, a pressed flower, a letter you received. Write in recipes and songs you make up and codes you invent.

THE PATROL SYSTEM AND HOW IT WORKS

One thing you will notice about Guides is that everyone is important, and everyone has a chance to make her ideas heard.

If you were a Brownie you should remember the Brownie Pow-wow, where you talked about what you would like to do, and how to plan Ventures and things.

In Guides we work together in Patrols which are small enough to let everyone have a say, with a Patrol Leader who makes sure everyone says something.

When a Patrol gets together to talk about and decide things (what they want to do, how much the subs should be, where they would like to camp or something like that) it is called a **Patrol-in-Council**.

The Patrol Leader listens to everyone's ideas, and helps the Patrol make its mind up, then takes all the ideas to another meeting of all the Patrol Leaders, Guiders and Young Leaders, called the **Patrol Leaders' Council**.

Guiding is run **democratically**, which means it is run by everyone who belongs to it. In Guiding everybody can have a say, whether it is in choosing games and Good Turns or helping to test a handbook like this before it is printed. (Ask your Guider to find out about Guiding things and how you can help make decisions outside your unit.)

YOUR PATROL LEADER

Each Patrol chooses its own Patrol Leader. When elections for Patrol Leader come up your Company could get together to talk about what the perfect Patrol Leader would be like.

Which of these things should a Patrol Leader be?
(Put a tick or cross in the boxes)

Friendly □
Kind □ Good at everything □
Well-organized □ A good listener □ Someone you can trust □ Bossy □ Someone who gives others the chance to lead □ Keen □ Oldest girl in Patrol □ Best person for the job □ Good at some things but not at others □ Full of good ideas □ Should have lots of badges □ It depends on the Patrol □

WHAT ELSE?

Make a list of some of the things you think a Patrol Leader should be, and also a list of suggestions for things she should try not to be.

THE PATROL LEADER'S JOB

Each Company asks its Patrol Leaders to do different things, but the sort of things she might do are:
● **organize the Patrol**
● **help new members**
● **make sure that someone keeps records of subscriptions and attendance for the Guides in her Patrol**
● **know how each member of her Patrol is getting on**
● **lead discussions in Patrol-in-**

Council meetings and make sure everyone has a say
● make sure someone is responsible for the Patrol corner and Patrol box
● represent her Patrol at the Patrol Leaders' Council
● tell the Patrol what the PLC decides.

SHARED LEADERSHIP

The best leaders share their tasks with others. Your Patrol Leader is responsible for seeing that things get done, but that doesn't mean she has to do them all by herself! Everyone in the Patrol is part of the 'team', and everyone helping the Patrol Leader to get things done is what really makes it work.

The Patrol Leader shares the leadership with her Second.

YOUR PATROL SECOND

The Patrol Leader chooses the **Patrol Second**. She should choose someone she knows she can get on well with and who will be respected and liked by the other girls in the Patrol. The Patrol Second takes the Patrol Leader's place when the Patrol Leader is not there.

Seconds know that they will not automatically become the next Patrol Leader, because the Patrol has to elect their new PL. When a Patrol Leader leaves or there are elections, the new Patrol Leader chooses her own Second.

THE PATROL-IN-COUNCIL

You can have a Patrol-in-Council meeting whenever you want to, to talk about anything you like, but especially:
● what you would like to do as a Patrol
● whether you would like to work for an Interest Badge, a Patrol Interest Pennant or a Patrol Purpose Patch together
● Patrol things, like electing a PL or arranging a Promise Ceremony or buying Patrol equipment
● looking back at things you have done.

Patrol-in-Council meetings are also held before and after the Patrol Leaders' Council. Before the Patrol Leaders' Council meets each Patrol talks about the things the PLC wants to discuss, such as camp, District events, subscriptions, Good Turns or fund raising. The Patrol Leader listens to everyone's ideas and makes notes so that she can remember what the Patrol felt (or she might ask a Patrol Secretary to do this). After the PLC, your Patrol Leader will tell the Patrol about the decisions it made.

TAKING NOTES

THE PATROL LEADERS' COUNCIL (PLC)

Your Company runs itself through the Patrol Leaders' Council, which is made up of all the Patrol Leaders, your Guiders and Young Leaders if you have them. Sometimes the PLC invites other people like Ranger Guides or Brownie Guiders if a special event is planned. In some units the Seconds may be invited occasionally.

The Patrol Leaders represent their Patrols on the PLC. The PLC may meet every term, once a month or whenever it needs to. At the meeting, everyone has a say in planning the Company's programme, making sure that Patrol plans fit in with one another and deciding on activities the Company will do together. The PLC also decides whether to award Trefoil Badges or Patrol Purpose Patches and recommends Guides who want to help with Brownies as Pack Leaders.

PATROL MEETINGS

Patrol meetings are different from Patrol-in-Council meetings. Patrol meetings are when the Patrol gets together for a cookout, to go swimming, to rehearse an item for a concert, to do things for an Interest Badge or PIP, in fact any time when the Patrol members get together outside a unit meeting.

The best way to make Patrol meetings fun is for everyone in the Patrol to work to keep the meeting running smoothly and you can do this by sharing the leadership.

Everyone in your Patrol should:
- find out what they and the others want or need to do
- help to carry out plans that have been made
- encourage suggestions and ask questions
- be fair and co-operate with one another.

This story shows how people can share leadership in groups and take on responsible roles.

THE ROBIN'S PATROL MEETING

The Robins had got together to mark their Patrol equipment for camp. Joanne arrived early, so she went to get the key of the store from the caretaker and when the rest of the Patrol arrived she had got out some of the things they would need. Nicky began to help Joanne while Kim and Helen began to spread things out ready to be painted.

When Rachel arrived, though, she had forgotten the paint she

was supposed to bring. Helen rolled her eyes and said 'Oh no – we can't do anything without the paint!' Kim doesn't like arguments, so she jumped in to stop things getting out of hand. She said perhaps Rachel could go back home with her to collect the paint. Meanwhile Nicky had noticed that some of the things needed to be a bit cleaner before they were marked so they all washed them while they were waiting for the paint.

When Rachel and Kim came back, they brought some 'Robins' stickers that Rachel had made at home for the Patrol camp box, and Kim brought some biscuits and squash to have at teatime.

Could you tell from the story who was the Patrol Leader?
– Joanne thought ahead to save the Patrol time.
– Kim made peace when people might have started to blame Rachel, and brought some refreshments to help the work along.
– Nicky spotted a job that needed doing.
– Rachel had made some stickers for the whole Patrol.
– Helen helped the Patrol, even though she lost her temper for a moment.

How many of these ideas apply to people in your Patrol?

In the . . . . Patrol, we have people who:

plan ahead	☐
are enthusiastic	☐
understand each other's point of view	☐
help each other	☐
organize	☐
gather information	☐
share information with others	☐
see when there's a problem and try to solve it	☐
are fair to each other	☐
stick together when a problem arises	☐
help others to co-operate	☐
show that they accept others	☐
show respect for others	☐
keep the peace	☐
keep track of time	☐
inspire each other	☐
think clearly	☐
work hard	☐
show imagination	☐
evaluate	☐

Don't worry about negative things you may think of – if you work on the good things, the bad ones will not seem so awful!

ROBIN

GET TO KNOW YOUR PATROL

☐ Have a quiz about who's good at what. You could give out Patrol jobs as a result of this.

☐ If possible, have Patrol meetings in each other's homes.

☐ Ask everyone's mother or father to come to a Patrol meeting.

☐ Have a beautiful baby competition. All bring along photos of yourselves as babies – can everyone work out who is who?

☐ Have one minute talks on 'Me' by each member of the Patrol (you could introduce yourself, describe your family, how many brothers and sisters you have, if you have any pets, what school you go to, your faith, your favourite things, etc).

☐ Have a blind obstacle race. Ask your Guider or challenge another Patrol to set up a blind obstacle race for you in your meeting place. Each member of the Patrol in turn takes another member of the Patrol round it, blindfolded.

MAKING PLANS

What can you do at Patrol meetings or during Patrol Time in your unit meeting? You'll find lots of ideas for activities from your own ideas and imagination, the pages of this Handbook and *GUIDE PATROL* magazine.

There are also lots of books and activity packs published by the GGA – you can get a catalogue by writing to: The GGA Trading Service, Atlantic Street, Broadheath, Altrincham, Cheshire WA14 5EQ. Your Guiders and other Guides are also a good source of ideas.

You can:
- work for a Patrol Interest Pennant/Patrol Purpose Patch
- do an Interest Badge as a Patrol
- use a Patrol activity to help with an Interest Badge or a Trefoil Badge
- practise skills
- play games
- discuss items for the Patrol Leaders' Council.

A GUIDE MAKES GOOD USE OF HER TIME...

Here are some simple ways to make sure that the time your Patrol spends together isn't wasted.

1. IDEAS

Banish those 'what can we do now?' blues by always having a foolproof supply of good ideas.

- **Brainstorm** – everyone in the Patrol should say what she would like to do, both as a Patrol and in the unit. One of the Patrol should write down all the ideas, even if they're really silly, and no one should make any comments about the ideas at all – just concentrate on getting everyone's ideas down on paper. If you have a computer with a word-processing system, this is a good reason to use it!

- **Have a Patrol ideas box** – use a shoebox with a hole in the top to post ideas into whenever they happen – when anyone says 'Let's…' or 'I wish we could…' or 'Why don't we…' If you can't do it now, save it for later, and when you are looking for ideas, look in the box!

- **Talk about the things you've done in the past year or so** – What would you like

to do again? Is there anything you'd like to do better? Is there a badge or Pennant you could work for?

2. WEED OUT AND DECIDE

When you've got your ideas, you need to sort them out. Look at the list and sort them into headings like this:

Can do at Guides
Make conservation poster
Plan Thinking Day
Tracking signs

Weekend
Hike to beach and cookout

Out of doors
Canoeing
Tracking

Combine things which are similar, and put things which you know you can't do just yet on one side – you might be able to include them next time.

If there are things you don't know much about, ask the person whose idea it was to find out more for the next meeting and pencil it in (or put it in brackets if it's on screen).

Remember that some things will cost money – some much more than others – will you need to raise any money for equipment, fares, etc?

Add things you know about from the PLC: District swimming gala, Guide Camp Permit weekend run by Division, unit visit to fire station, etc.

When you have organized your list you are ready to set out a programme for the next month or so or longer.

JANUARY 12	MAKING RECRUITMENT POSTERS
JANUARY 19	
JANUARY 26	PARENT'S EVENING / HOSTESS BADGE
JANUARY 28	COUNTY CRAFT DAY AT KNIGHTON
FEBRUARY 2	UNIT VISIT TO AMBULANCE STATION
FEBRUARY 9	
FEBRUARY 16	PLANNING OUR ACTIVITY FOR TD PARTY
FEBRUARY 21	PATROL COOKING MEETING AT MELANIE'S
FEBRUARY 22	THINKING DAY PARTY WITH 25th GUIDES
MARCH 1	
MARCH 2	SKATING AT VICTORIA SPORTS CENTRE
MARCH 8	MAP AND COMPASS
MARCH 15	EVERYONE BRING HIKING THINGS FOR CHECKING
HOLIDAY !	HIKE TO SALTERFORD WITH GUIDER

3. PROGRAMME PLANNING

The Scarlet Pimpernel Patrol planned their programme like this:

First they made a list of dates of Company meetings:

a. Then the Scarlet Pimpernels added some of the things from their lists which had specific dates.

b. Then they put down some of the things from the 'things to do at a Company meeting' list.

c. Then they decided to fit in a Patrol outing and voted on what to do – skating or swimming at the sports centre.

d. They also decided that they would need to have a Patrol meeting at home to cook for Thinking Day, so they put one in for the night before their meeting on the 22nd.

This still left some spaces but they decided to fill these in closer to the time, in case some of the activities ran over into the next week.

4. MAKE SURE IT HAPPENS!

It's easy to spend time thinking of things to do and setting out your programme, but the Patrol will have to keep on its toes to make sure that everything happens!

For every activity you need to plan in more detail and decide who is doing what:
- **when, where and what time**
- **who is bringing equipment**
- **who is buying things you will need**
- **who will keep your Guider informed**
- **who has anything specific to do before, during or after.**

If everyone is involved, and everyone has a special job to do, then the activity is more likely to go well. Make sure that the same person doesn't always have to do the jobs nobody likes – share them out so that everyone has a go.

You could write out the things needed for each meeting. Taking the hike as an example:

(You could use a word processor to make up your own planning sheets!)

Challenge Hiking   **Date** 15/3

Going   Claire, Kate, Lailani, Megan and Vicky.

Aims/plans   To learn over two meetings how to use a map and compass and to plan properly for a hike on Saturday 2 April.

First week:

We need:	Who will bring:
Silva compass	Claire
2 maps	Kate and Megan
Guide Handbook	everyone

Help needed: Claire to ask her sister Jane, a Ranger, to come to advise. Guider to lend two compasses and a map.

Second week:

We need:	Who will bring:
clothing and kit for hike	everyone
first aid kit	Vicky
finalize route	everyone
permission to go	everyone
to leave details for:	
parents	everyone
Guider	Claire
Thank you letter to Jane	Lailani

Help needed: Ask Guider to check our kit, the route and our first aid kit.

LOOK BACK

After any activity you should look back at what you did to see what was good, what was bad, what could have been better, and where your planning and preparation paid off.

Did you enjoy it?
Did you cope with everything?
What would you have done differently?
How many people felt that they learnt anything?
Would you do it again?

Make a note of anything you need to remember for next time and build on the things you have done.

★ HIKING ★

PATROL FINANCE

Where do your subs go? Well, for a start, your unit needs money for books, badges, craft materials,

camping and other equipment, maybe for rent and heating, and whatever else the unit needs. In addition, everyone in a Guide unit pays a subscription every year to the Girl Guides Association, to help pay for all of the things provided by

Commonwealth Headquarters:
● training for Guiders
● developing ideas for new badges
● producing books and magazines
● looking after camp sites and training centres
● keeping in touch with Guide Associations around the world

PASSPORT

● insurance
● looking after British Guides in Foreign Countries
● and all sorts of other things

Your District, Division, County and Country or Region also need money to help run Guiding in your area.

Your PLC will decide how all these things are paid for. In some units all the Guides pay a weekly, monthly or termly subscription to cover everything, while in others the GGA subscription is paid in a lump sum separately from the unit money. Your Company can pick any method that suits it, as long as everyone feels it is fair.

However, as well as this, your Patrol will find it needs money to carry out all the exciting activities you want to do. One way to raise the money the Patrol needs is to ask everyone to pay a small amount to the Patrol Treasurer each week. Another way is to pay an amount to cover the costs of each activity as it happens, although that can mean that you don't have spare money in the kitty to pay for everyday things like stamps and squash.

Decide how much contributions will be by:
● looking at your programme and deciding how much money you are likely to need
● deciding whether you need any new Patrol equipment
● what Patrol members can

afford
- looking at ways of fund raising
- making sure everyone feels the amount you choose is fair.

It's a good idea to look at Patrol subs regularly and raise or lower them if necessary.

To keep track of money paid in and spent your Patrol will need an account book. Here is one simple method for keeping Patrol accounts:

Date	Income £ p	Expenditure £ p

The treasurer should show the Patrol the accounts at Patrol-in-Council meetings and once a year at least to your Guider or the Patrol Leaders' Council.

If your Patrol subs are set at the right level, you should never have lots of money sitting around in a piggy bank – it should really be spent on what the Patrol needs soon after it

comes in.

If you are fund raising or saving up for a special event it is probably safer to keep larger sums of money with your Guider, but make sure you keep proper accounts of where it is in your book.

MONEY MAKING

Earning money can be fun if everyone in the Patrol does her bit. Follow the steps for making plans, talk to your Guider about it, have plenty of time to prepare and try to provide the very best goods or service for the price you are asking.

Money spinners
Sales: jumble, bring and buy, car boot, sale of work.
Stalls: crafts, tree decorations, plants, produce, soft toys.
Home-made specialities: cakes, biscuits, sweets, herbal preparations.
Collections: waste paper, aluminium cans and foil.
Service: car wash team, spring clean a house, gardening, bike repairs, pet minding, set up a crèche at a fête.
Catering: breakfasts, coffee evenings, hot dog stalls
Whatever you do, you should make it safe (no house-to-house collections) and legal (no one under 16 may rattle a tin in a street collection). Always check beforehand with your Guider.

This chapter contains just a few ideas for things you can do as a Patrol. You can plan lots more activities at your Patrol meetings – and then get on and do them!

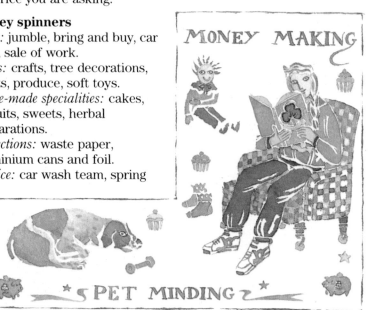

3

'*Today is the first day of the rest of your life!*'

Are you ready? Our motto

is 'Be Prepared'

3

– and in Guiding you can learn

to look after yourself and others

so that you are prepared for anything

that may

happen in

your life.

DIET
SHEET

FIT FOR ANYTHING

There's nothing like looking good to make you feel good about yourself – not by wearing the latest fashions but by being as healthy as you can and learning to look after yourself so that you stay healthy.

HAIR

Let's start at the top:

Healthy hair comes from a healthy scalp, not bottles or packets. The state of your hair is often a reflection of your health – if your diet is unbalanced your hair could go lank, brittle and dull. Shampoo your hair as often as it needs it and massage your scalp at the same time.

In your Patrol, look at the different types of hair you have – oily, normal or dry, how often you have to wash it and what kinds of shampoos and conditioners work best for you.

At a Patrol meeting, wash each other's hair so you could wash the hair of someone who couldn't do it herself.

Or look through magazines and try styling your hair in different ways. Try using different clips, benders, bands and styling techniques to turn your haircut into something a bit different.

Make your own hair decorations using plain clips or bands as a base. Plait ribbons into your hair if it's long enough. If you have short hair which is difficult to do anything with, why not try transforming an old hat – sew loads of different coloured buttons to a beret or tie a length of soft lace or netting over a straw hat. Again, look in magazines for ideas.

Invite a hair stylist to talk to your Patrol and show you some of the things you can do with your hair.

TEETH

Plaque is the real enemy when it comes to keeping your teeth healthy. Plaque is a mixture of saliva, bacteria and tiny particles of food which clings to your teeth. If you don't clean it away by brushing your teeth thoroughly it causes decay and gum disease.

Find out from your dentist or dental hygienist how to brush properly – a quick sloosh round isn't good enough! Dental floss is also useful for removing bits of food stuck between your teeth and it's a good idea to use it once or twice a week.

Look after your teeth – follow this Tooth and Gum Code:

1. Brush your teeth after meals.
2. Steer clear of sweet sticky food like chocolate, toffee, chewing gum and fizzy drinks. These stick to your teeth and help bacteria to make your teeth decay.
3. Try not to eat between meals, but if you must, eat things like carrots, nuts and apples
4. In general, the longer food stays in your mouth, (say, if you're sucking a gobstopper) the more damage it does. Fizzy drinks, even swallowed straight away are incredibly bad for your teeth because they contain sugar which sticks to your teeth for ages.
5. Visit your dentist regularly for check-ups.

If you are under 18 dental care is free so, if you haven't been to the dentist for a while, find out from your friends who they recommend, gather up your courage – and go! If you're under 16 you'll have to get one of your parents to sign a form which the receptionist will give you.

SKIN

Skin is pretty wonderful stuff. Your skin protects your body from all sorts of things like sunlight, dirt, germs and water. It gets rid of waste through sweat, allows you to feel the sensations of touch, pain and heat and it controls your body temperature. It stretches and folds, and is a mirror of your general health. Although it's quite tough, skin does need looking after!

To keep your skin healthy you've got to keep it clean:

1. Your face and hands get grubbier than the rest of your body because they're uncovered most of the time. You should wash them several times a day. Always wash hands after going to the toilet and if you have spots, try to keep your hands off them!
2. Using a mild cleansing bar is often gentler on the face than soap and will help to get rid of spots. If you wear make-up it's especially important to use a cleanser to remove it all.

3. Moisturisers keep your skin supple by keeping moisture in. Use them after washing and cleansing.
4. Strong sunshine can be bad for skin – use a sunscreen if you can and moisturise afterwards.

EATING WELL

How often do you get a chance to decide what you're going to eat? Breakfast? Packed lunch at school? School dinner? At home? Do you choose the things you like all the time, or do you remember that 'you are what you eat' and balance the things you like with the things you know are good for you?

A BALANCED DIET

Food is your body's fuel, in the same way that dry wood is fuel for a fire at camp. But what happens if you try to keep your fire going with other things? Use paper, and other things which flare up or burn quickly, and after a while you'll have a heap of flaky ash and a fire with no heat, which is absolutely no good at all for cooking your Patrol's tea!

In the same way, if you keep filling yourself with the wrong sort of food, or eat things which your body can't use properly, you'll find that you get tired, and ill, and worn out, and just like the camp fire you'll be no good for doing anything useful!

So the answer is to eat a combination of different foods that your body can use as fuel to keep you breathing, growing, moving, thinking, and doing everything else you throw at it! Every day you should eat something from each of these groups.

·Fat·

Fats – also for energy, fats help to transport vitamins around your body to where they are needed, and promote healthy skin. There are two types – saturated and polyunsaturated. Too much saturated fat can lead to a higher risk of heart disease when you get older, so include more things like skimmed or low-fat milk and cheese, lean meats and polyunsaturated margarine in your diet.

·Carbohydrate·

·Protein·

If you eat something from each group, you'll be making sure your body is supplied with:
Protein – to help your body grow and repair itself

Carbohydrates – for energy and to help digest other foods, plus roughage. Beware of too much sugar, which can lead to obesity and tooth decay!

·Fibre·

Fibre (or roughage) – to help your digestive system get rid of waste products.

Your body also needs minerals and vitamins. **Minerals** are things like iron, which helps to form red blood cells; calcium, which is needed for strong bones and teeth; sodium, which regulates your body temperature; fluoride; potassium and zinc. **Vitamins** are found in different fresh foods and do things like helping eyes to work properly (Vitamin A), or for healthy skin (Vitamin C).

FOOD FOR THOUGHT

Water is vital for life – that means people need a reliable supply of clean drinking water to live and be healthy. Water makes up two-thirds of your body, and you lose it through your skin and when you go to the toilet, so you need to replace the fluid you lose by drinking six to eight cups of fluid per day – more in hot weather. Plain water is better for you than other drinks which have substances in them which can affect your body.

If you can, eat three meals a day.

Try not to eat between meals – but if you must, stick to healthy snacks such as raw carrot sticks, raisins and nuts.

Don't skip meals – it starves your body of nutrients and makes you grab the nearest junk food to stave off hunger pangs.

Cooking methods can help: grill, don't fry; steam, don't boil. Overcooking doesn't just spoil food – it can destroy vitamins and a lot of the nutritive value.

'Convenience' food doesn't mean 'junk' food – fresh fruit is about as convenient as you can get! Dried, frozen and unsweetened tinned foods can also be fresher than raw foods which have been hanging around in the fridge for a week.

Things to do as a Patrol

☐ Write down everything you can remember that you have eaten today or in the past week. Is it a balanced diet? Can you improve it using the ideas above.

♣Given a sum of money (maybe £1 for each member of the Patrol) shop for and cook a healthy meal.

☐ Make a Top of the Pops food chart. Do a survey of everyone's favourite foods. Do they like 'healthy eating'? Talk about everyone's likes and dislikes.

♣Make a vegetarian meal.

☐ Have a milk-tasting session – see which ones your Patrol prefers. Make a cup of tea and decide how you like it with different kinds of milk e.g. pasteurized, semi-skimmed, soya, or even with no milk at all!

☐ Look at different diets in your Patrol, or diets people might follow for cultural or ethical reasons e.g. halal, kosher, vegetarian, vegan. Find out what these terms mean, what types of food they include and other rules different communities have for eating.

☐ Find out where to buy some of these foods and try them out.

☐ Look at different diets people follow for medical reasons e.g. low fat, gluten free, allergies. What do food companies do to help? What more could they do?

☐ Think about the last three ideas and see how you would make them work at Guide camp or another event.

☐ Have a 'healthy eating' sale of goodies for your next fund-raising event.

☐ Plan a three-course meal from a list of ingredients given to you by your Guider.

☐ Plan the menu for your next day out using the ideas on nutrition above.

☐ Have a 'super sandwich' evening – bring different types of bread and lots of fillings and make sandwiches for different occasions: school; a hike; a wedding; a festival; Thinking Day; a barbecue; a beach party; you can think of others! Use your imagination to create the right fillings for the occasion!

☐ Find out about diets for young people in developing countries. How do they compare with yours? Are they any healthier?

FITNESS MATTERS

You probably take your fitness for granted. You get all the exercise you need at school, right?

Wrong. Most young people today are unfit. Surveys have shown that they spend more time watching TV and sitting still than they spend moving. When you were young, you probably played lots of active games, but as you get older you start to enjoy sitting talking more, and more commitments at school can mean you spend more time in class and less time being active.

So what? Well, regular exercise is an important way of becoming physically fit. It helps you to develop flexibility, strength and stamina. Your body is a complicated machine for breathing, moving and thinking, and to do all the things you ask it to, it needs to be kept in the best possible condition.

Exercise is not boring – it'll help you make friends, feel stronger, be happier and live longer! What it won't do is make you thinner – at least not all by itself – but it will help you to stand and move with better posture, so that you'll feel leaner and look healthier, even if you feel you might not be the ideal shape or size!

The games periods you have at school will help keep you fit, especially if you really throw yourself into them. But even if you hate games you can still be fit – swimming, walking briskly and dancing are good ways of exercising.

Think about active sports such as netball, hockey, football, running, dancing to pop music, skating, swimming and cycling. These build up endurance and help to strengthen your heart and lungs. For flexibility you could try gymnastics, aerobics, yoga, the martial arts and ballet. If you have a medical condition, then obviously you shouldn't do anything to make it worse, but talk to your doctor about ways of keeping fit.

No matter what activity you do, always give your muscles and joints time to get going. Warming up means just that: the body temperature rises and the fluid around the joints flows more easily making movement easier. Start at the head and shoulders and work down the body.

Head turns

Chin to chest

Pelvis rotation

Shoulder shrugs

Feet apart, knees relaxed, bottom pointing down.

Side bends

Arm circles

Knee lifts

Do these to the front and to the sides. Add arm movements to get your whole body moving.

Elbow circles

Go straight to the side, holding your pelvis straight. Bottom down, knees relaxed.

Stretch and relax

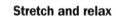

STRETCHES

You should stretch before and after exercising to avoid injuries, such as a pulled muscle. Cool down afterwards by gently stretching the muscles you have been using in your exercises.

THE WORK-OUT

A work-out is an exercise routine you plan ahead, using more vigorous exercises. It can last around 15–20 minutes, depending on your energy! Plan a work-out with your Patrol or with a friend, and do it at a Patrol meeting. Use a record with a strong rhythm to help you exercise.

Warm up and stretch
(10 minutes)

The work-out (20 minutes) – any activity you like, at a pace to make you slightly breathless. If you are a little overweight to start with, don't try to do too much too soon and remember your extra weight means you will burn more calories than someone who is her ideal weight.

Final stretch and relax

(5 minutes) – gently stretch the muscles you have just worked. Finish by lying really limp with your eyes closed.

If you aren't used to exercising your muscles, you may feel a little sore. Don't overdo it. Work at your own pace and – most important – **if it hurts or if you become breathless stop and rest!** It is better to exercise regularly and not to overdo it at first.

Other exercise activities to try:

Walk or run up stairs rather than taking the lift.

Walk instead of accepting a ride in the car or taking the bus; or get off a stop or two early (but don't do this if it might be unsafe, e.g. along an empty road, late at night or on your own).

Choose to do active things with your free time. Encourage your Patrol to go swimming, cycling, dancing or skating so that your social life will keep you fit.

Try a new sport with your Patrol or a friend.

Set yourself an exercise target – a set number of lengths to swim, a time to run a distance, a distance to throw.

Make up your own routine for keeping fit including a warm-up, work-out and cool-down. Do this routine three times a week for one month – a fitness challenge! How do you feel at the end of that month?

Use a door frame to help you stretch or a broom handle.

CLOTHES LINES...

What you wear can reflect the type of person you are and how you feel about yourself. Here are some tips on how to look after your clothes and keep yourself looking good.

WHICH?

There's nothing like going out to do your own shopping and buying your own things with your friends. But it's not always easy to choose – how often have you spent your hard-saved pounds on a big mistake, or been talked into something you knew at the time you'd never wear or use!

Making choices is a part of getting ready for life. (Making mistakes is part of making choices!) Maybe other people buy your clothes and other things for you at the moment but you probably get a word in edgeways. Later on you'll be making your own decisions about what to wear, what to do, what to eat (maybe not just for yourself but for others, too). So get ready for choices by starting now.

You've saved your birthday money, you're out with your best friend, you spot a really brilliant top.

Stop right there! Don't just grab it and head for the 'please pay here' signs. Ask some questions…

● **Will it wash?** (Look at the label. If it says 'dry clean only', do you really want the hassle?)
● **Is it well made?** (Look at the seams and the details. Are the buttons coming off already?)
● **Will it go with anything else?** (If the answer is 'no' or even 'only my best jeans', think hard. Do you really want something you can't wear very often?)
● **Is the colour right?** Are you the right shape for it? (Ask your friends to be honest – and be honest with yourself, too!)
● **Will you still like it in three weeks?** (Difficult, this one – you need to ask yourself why you're buying it in the first place!)

WHAT'S IN YOUR WARDROBE?

Take some time to sort out your wardrobe. Clear a space and spread out all your clothes. Pass on things you've grown out of to younger sisters, relatives or to a charity shop. Hang up skirts, dresses and trousers (and shirts if you have space). Fold T-shirts and jumpers and keep them on shelves or in drawers. Keep underwear together. Look at all your socks and tights – mend holes or throw out any beyond repair.

Line shelves and drawers with paper (bright wrapping paper is fun) and keep clothes smelling fresh with lavender bags and scented soaps (the ones you can't use because they bring you out in spots).

LOOK AFTER YOUR CLOTHES

Clothes that are washed regularly last longer, smell fresher, feel better. Most clothes can be washed in a machine, but some are more delicate and need hand washing, while other fabrics have special finishes and so have to be dry cleaned. Learn how to wash your own clothes now so that you don't make mistakes later!

First check the care labels for your clothes. They're in code!

Find out what these symbols mean.

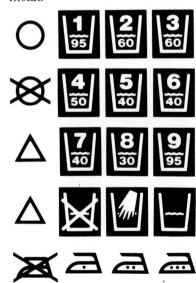

Handwash:
Dissolve powder/ liquid in water

Immerse garment

Rub gently, 'agitate'!

Squeeze water out

Rinse in clean water two or three times until all soap is gone

Machine wash:
Sort washing into heaps of all the same label

Empty pockets – paper hankies ruin the wash and coins can damage the machine

Load machine

Set programme or time

Load powder/ liquid (see packet for amount) Switch on Don't put your

hand in the machine while it's working!

PullOn PushOFF

If you have a twin-tub you'll need to rinse and spin after the main wash.

Unload when the machine stops and hang to dry straight away.

Dry cleaning

Try different local dry-cleaners until you find one you like.

Stains

Sometimes you'll have to treat stains before the wash. You can buy special removers for particular stains, or you can try treating them with things you can find around the house. Find out from your local library ways of removing stains using household goods.

how effective the different cleaners are at shifting the stains. See if soaking before washing helps.

Are 'ecologically sound' washing powders and liquids as effective as others? How ecological are they?

If your Patrol wear neckerchiefs, wash, dry, iron and freshly roll them all. There's no excuse for a neckerchief like a dishrag!

DASHING AWAY...

Ironing – the bane of life! Can you iron your own shirts? Make yourself popular at home by taking over your own ironing whenever you can.

As a Patrol:
☐ Experiment with different washing powders or liquids. Cut an old cotton sheet into squares and stain them with different things (eg blood, tomato sauce, coffee, mud, grass, felt-tipped pen, grease, oil, etc). Then see

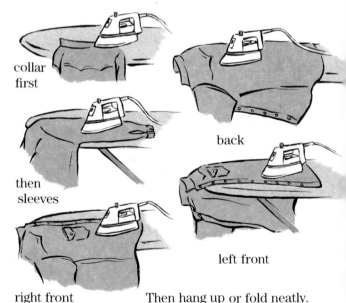

collar first

then sleeves

right front

back

left front

Then hang up or fold neatly.

46

RUNNING REPAIRS

Even if you absolutely hate needlework at school, there's no denying that it's useful to know how to do your own running repairs to clothes.

Hem coming down?
Catch it up again with tiny stitches.

Buttons falling off?
Sew back on securely.

Seam coming apart?
Back stitch – stronger than running stitch.

Fraying fabric?
Use a sewing machine and oversew – or use blanket stitch to oversew.

SEWING STYLE

Making your own clothes can be fun – and cheaper than buying! Try using these basic stitches to make a tube skirt. You can adapt the instructions to make a tube-shaped top or leg-warmers.

You will need: paper and pencil to make a pattern with, stretch fabric, synthetic thread, scissors, tape measure, elastic, safety pins, ballpoint pins and needles

1. To calculate the width of the material measure your hips and add 8cm to this measurement so that you can walk in your skirt! The length of fabric you will need is the measurement from your waist to where you want the skirt to end plus 6cm for the seam.
2. To make the pattern: on a sheet of paper draw a rectangle with sides of the right length and width and cut it out.
3. Using the ballpoint pins pin the pattern on to the fabric and cut around it. The fabric should stretch across the width, not the length.

4.

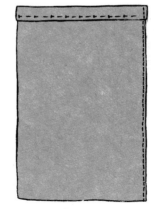

fold 1cm

Sew down the seam using backstitch if hand sewing or a narrow zigzag if using a sewing machine.

2cm

5.

1cm

Sew with back stitch.

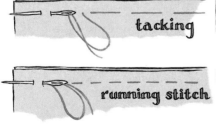

tacking

running stitch

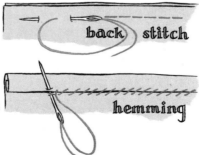

back stitch

hemming

Fasten the safety pin to one end of the elastic and feed it through the waistband. Then pin the two ends of the elastic together and try on for size. Adjust to the right size and cut off the excess elastic. Sew the two ends together and remove the safety pin. Sew up the hem opening.

6. Try on the skirt and ask a friend to pin up the hem at the right length. Sew carefully round the hem and iron to finish.

Find an old container to keep your sewing equipment in and decorate it with paint or paper to make it your own.

KNITTING

Knitting is a great way to make your own clothes; from simple scarves to complicated patterned jumpers. Find out how to knit from a friend or a craft book (look in your local library). Look out for the easier patterns which use big needles (about 4 mm) and thick (double-knitting) yarn. Lots of magazines have free knitting patterns in them and also give you tips about how to make up the garment.

Ideas:

☐ Design and print a T-shirt.
☐ Make a camp blanket.
☐ Learn how to load and use a washing machine. Remember to sort your washing into piles first according to the cleaning instructions.
☐ Look on the supermarket shelves and find out which products are the right ones for handwashing.
☐ Plan a wardrobe for travelling around the world. Why did you choose each item?

CHOICES FOR HEALTH

Eating a balanced diet, keeping hair, skin and hands clean, looking after your possessions – they're ways of looking good and feeling fit. But there are times when you'll be faced with other situations where you'll need to make your own choices for health – about things like smoking, alcohol, drugs and looking after your own body 'space'.

WHAT ARE THE EFFECTS OF SMOKING?

● Cigarettes stain your fingers and teeth yellow.

● The smell of cigarette smoke hangs around your clothes, your hair, your breath – anyone can tell when someone who smokes walks into the room!

● If you smoke, your senses of smell and taste are 'blocked' and you find you can't smell or taste your favourite food any more.

● Smoking near someone who doesn't smoke isn't just rude – it can actually harm them!

● Someone who smokes gets to depend on the nicotine in cigarettes. Although they say that they could give up smoking any time they wanted to, when they try they find they can't –

they've become addicted.

● A woman who smokes when she is pregnant can actually harm the baby inside her.

● Smoking can make you ill – it can make you more likely to have heart disease, lung cancer and other illnesses. Some of them can kill you.

So why do people smoke?

IT'S THE ONLY TIME I GET ANY PEACE

EVERYONE DOES IT – THEY'D LAUGH IF I REFUSED

MY FRIENDS DO

IT CALMS ME DOWN

I CAN'T STOP

IT KEEPS MY WEIGHT DOWN

Some people start smoking because they don't want to stand out from the crowd – they're frightened to say 'no'. How can you stand up for your own views?

Some people smoke because they're addicted to the nicotine. If they try to stop, they find themselves getting ratty, tense and impatient. Sometimes they eat more because they need to do something with their hands (and of course their taste buds recover so they can enjoy food more as well!).

Some people smoke because they say it keeps their weight down. Well, it certainly can stop you enjoying food, but if you're not eating, or you're eating less because you're smoking, you probably aren't getting the balanced diet you need to grow. You might not put weight on, but you won't look particularly good, because you won't be healthy!

Some people smoke because it gives them a chance to sit down in peace for a minute (especially busy adults!). The nicotine in the cigarettes is a drug which helps people relax, and busy or worried people often use their smoking to make them feel better. The cigarettes don't make the problem go away, or help the person solve it – it's still there when the nicotine wears off! If you know someone who smokes because they are stressed, how can you help them to rely less on cigarettes to ease their problems?

WE'RE GOING TO TRY TO STOP SMOKING TOGETHER – IT'LL BE EASIER IF WE HELP EACH OTHER

WHAT ABOUT ALCOHOL?

Alcohol on its own is a colourless substance, and not many people drink it on its own. But lots of people – and not just adults – drink things with alcohol in them – perhaps they enjoy wine with meals or (over-18s only) enjoy a beer at their local pub. As far as health is concerned, that's probably okay – a small amount of alcoholic drink now and again does no harm and can be enjoyable.

But ... alcohol is a drug which makes your brain work less well, so that your reactions are slower and you have less self-control. When people drink too much they can become dangerous (if they're driving a car) or violent (if they're arguing with someone).

You need to be able to make your own choice between:

not drinking at all

drinking sometimes

drinking too much, or for the wrong reasons

When people drink too much, other people can see them getting drunk, but what they can't see is the damage too much alcohol can do inside their bodies and minds. Too much drinking can cause: damage to the liver; stomach problems; brain damage; depression; vitamin deficiency; and other things. Some people get addicted to alcohol and this can mess up not just their bodies but their lives and those of their families as well.

Girls and women are more easily affected by alcoholic drinks than men because their body make-up is different – women have a lower proportion of body fluid to total weight than men, so when alcohol is spread around the body it stays more concentrated in women than in men (in men, the alcohol gets more 'diluted'). And, of course, if a woman who is pregnant drinks alcohol it passes through her bloodstream and shares the drink with the growing baby – which is not good for it at all!

Many people don't agree with drinking anything containing alcohol at all. They choose to be teetotal or abstainers, and when they go out they drink soft drinks like fruit juice. Some people choose not to drink alcohol for health reasons, some for religious reasons.

It is actually illegal for you to buy or serve alcohol in a pub, off-licence or supermarket until you are 18 years old, but you might find that people offer you drinks before that. So you need to think about it before it happens to be ready to make the choice.

Your decision about drinking alcohol will be based on lots of factors such as what your family and friends do or what your religious beliefs are. Here are some things to think about when you have made your choice:

Alcohol and nicotine are just two of the drugs that can damage your body. Your doctor sometimes gives you drugs in the form of medicines to help you when you are ill, so you know how they can affect your body. But, just as drugs can be used to affect the body in a good way, they can also be used (or misused), affecting the body in a bad way. Also, ordinary things (such as glue) can be used in a way which harms the body.

It might seem strange that anyone could deliberately do anything to cause themselves harm ... but when you read

If you choose to drink

- know the risks
- drink sensibly
- don't tease people who don't want to drink
- know the law

If you choose not to drink

- don't be talked into it
- don't apologize
- go out with friends who care about you
- plan what to say if offered a drink

the newspapers and watch the news on television you can see that there are lots of people like that. So why do they do it?

- because their friends do
- to avoid responsibility
- to run away from problems
- because they are unhappy

- for kicks
- because they are bored
- to hide problems
- and also because they can't stop – they've become addicted.

You might find yourself in a situation where people are sniffing glue, or even using drugs. If anyone offers you anything you think is suspicious, say **NO** politely but firmly and tell an adult you can trust – that's not 'telling tales'!

Patrol ideas
♣ Find out about the effects of abusing one of: alcohol; tobacco; solvents; drugs. Make up a TV advert encouraging young people to choose health.
☐ Make non-alcoholic cocktails.
☐ Act out how to say no in situations where you are offered alcohol or drugs.
☐ Help another person to give up or cut down on smoking (they must want to give up – they're not going to give up just because you're doing a challenge!)
☐ Invite a local person to talk to the unit about drug awareness – contact the police or your local Health Education Unit.
☐ Support 'No Smoking Day' or local Drug Awareness weeks.

☐ Make badges and posters.
☐ Talk about whether Guiders should smoke in front of Guides/at meetings/at camp. Discuss with the whole unit.
☐ Draw a large body shape (by drawing round someone) and find out how cigarettes, alcohol and other drugs affect the body. Mark the affected parts on your drawing.
☐ Discuss the cost of drugs – how might someone be forced to raise this money?
☐ Talk about drug abuse with an expert. What do various drugs and drug equipment look like? How can you tell if someone may be using drugs? Talk about what you would do if you suspected someone at school or Guides was trying drugs.
☐ Find out about the links between drug use and crime, young people committing suicide, and AIDS. What are the effects of drugs on both the user and his or her family and friends?

Find useful addresses in your local library.

LOOK AFTER YOURSELF!

You probably know about 'stranger danger' – not taking lifts, presents or money from people you don't know, and never going off with someone you don't know. Guiding involves getting involved with other people – like when you're out and about or giving service to others – but in this day and age it's best to make sure that contact with other people doesn't put you into danger. The same goes for everyday life, too – don't be unfriendly, but at the same time keep yourself safe.

You can avoid situations which might put you at risk:

- don't walk home alone – ask someone to collect you or walk with a group
- don't let people know that you're at home alone – don't answer the door or phone if you're not sure who's calling, or say things like 'Mum can't come to the phone at the moment, but she'll call you back when she's free'
- if you think you're being followed, go to the nearest shop, police station or house and tell an adult or phone home
- always tell your family where you're going, who with and what time you'll be back – then if you're delayed, phone home and tell people why (do you know how to make a reversed charge telephone call?)
- keep to busy roads and footpaths and avoid crossing waste ground, building sites or remote parks. At night keep to well-lit areas and avoid short cuts and being on your own
- if someone asks for directions, stay polite but don't get too close, especially to cars. Never get into a car to show someone the way.

If someone does try to molest you, take a step back. It gives you a momentary advantage. Scream and shout – make enough din to attract attention and confuse your attacker. Run away if you can. Tell your parents or a trusted adult at once. Don't let anyone tell you it doesn't matter – it does!

If you see something suspicious or think someone has tried to harm you, try to remember:
When did it happen?
What happened?
Where did it happen?
Who was there?

Try to remember what the person(s) looked like (male or female, height, weight, clothing, shoes and colour of hair, skin, and eyes). Also try to remember important details about the person's vehicle (registration number, colour and model).

IN YOUR PATROL...

Talk about and act out what do to in these situations. Try to think of more than one solution:
- A man knocks on your door. He says he has come to read the gas or electricity meter. What do you do?
- You are alone in the house when the phone rings. The caller asks if your parents are at home. What do you say?
- Someone comes to your door and asks to use your phone. What do you do?
- As you are walking home from school a stranger approaches and tells you one of your parents has had an accident. He has been sent to take you home. What would you do?
- An adult asks you to play a game and wants you to promise to keep it a secret. What should you do?

THINGS TO TRY FOR YOURSELF:

☐ Make up a Town Code (like the Country Code) for safety sense. Write it in verse or make a cartoon poster of it.
☐ Make up sketches to reinforce safety sense.
☐ Find out about Childline and the 'Just Say No' campaign.
☐ Make a list of useful information to keep at home. Include addresses/telephone numbers/any other information needed:
Local police station
Closest neighbours
Train and bus inquiries
Family doctor
Parents' work
School/s
Add any other important family numbers

POLITICS IS LIFE

It might be a few years yet before you'll be casting your vote but you can still take an interest in what's going on around you. 'Politics' can mean many things – political parties, Parliament, a new by-pass, Europe, local elections … it's a huge subject and some people get involved for life!

But politics isn't just protests and Prime Minister's Question Time! Politics is about people working out ways of living and that applies at every level from families to international communities of nations. In every society there are rules and guidelines for living and these are agreed (or imposed) by the people who live in it.

Think about your own family, and some of the 'rules' it has. How are these decided? Do you think they're fair? Are there things you'd like to change? How might you go about it?

There are probably rules at your school – how are they made? Is there a pupils' or students' committee? Are there things at school you can decide for yourself or does one person decide everything?

In Guiding there are politics – how your unit decides things like the amount of subs, or where to go for camp, or who's going to be Patrol Leader. These are things which should be discussed in your Patrols before your Patrol Leader goes to the Patrol Leaders' Council. Everyone in the GGA has a voice, from the youngest Rainbow Guide picking her favourite game to Rangers deciding how to raise and spend £500 on unit equipment.

In the UK, wherever you live you will have local councillors, a Member of Parliament and a Member of the European Parliament. These people are elected by other people aged 18 and over to represent them and help to run the community. Most councillors, MPs and MEPs belong to a political party although some are independent.

IDEAS

☐ Make politics work for you in your unit – make sure your Patrol Leaders' Council really works!

☐ Keep up with what's going on in the GGA by ordering a Patrol copy of *GUIDE PATROL* and make your own views known by writing a letter to the editor.

☐ Collect newspaper cuttings presenting different opinions on a political issue. Talk about them and your opinions with your Patrol.

☐ In your Patrol, hold a debate on an issue which is important to you. Ask one person to represent each side of the argument. Cast votes at the end to decide which side you agree with.

☐ Do you have a parish council? Does anyone on it represent the views of young people? If not, is there anything you can do about it?

☐ Find out about your local council – who your councillors are, which political parties they belong to, what their policies are. How does this affect you?

☐ In your Patrol talk about what you think the council should provide for the community. Find out what services are provided by your council. How are these paid for?

☐ Find out about a pressure group – what their aims are and how they hope to achieve them.

☐ Make a map of your area showing the boundaries of your local council ward, the area covered by the council, your parliamentary constituency and your European constituency.

☐ Watch or listen to political broadcasts by the major political parties on the radio and television and think/talk about who you would vote for.

☐ Find out about how the government is elected and who can vote. What sort of decisions does the government make and how do their actions affect your daily life?

☐ Compare the voting system in this country with the voting systems in other countries.

MONEY MANAGEMENT

Some girls get an allowance every month, some get pocket money on Fridays, some get money or things whenever they like, some don't get anything at all. Whatever you get, you'll know that you can only spend it once, so you need to know how to make the best of it. And if you don't get any regular pocket money, you might want to think about starting to earn your own (although there are age limits for being 'employed').

Write down everything you spend in a week – bus fares, food, Guide subs, magazines, etc.

Do you have to pay for it all out of your allowance or do things like bus fares and clothes come out of the general housekeeping? Do you get enough money to pay for the things you need? Is there enough left over to pay for the

things you'd like? Right, what are you going to save for, or do without?

Writing everything down and looking at it like this is the beginning of budgeting – working out how much money you have, and when and how to spend or save it.

Write your own budget and try to follow it for at least a month. Work out which are fixed expenses – things you have to pay for every day- and which are luxuries – things you don't need, but which you would like to buy. If you can't afford your luxuries, you'll have to think about what you want most and then do without for a while and save until you can afford it!

IDEAS

☐ Find out where your Guide subs go and what they pay for.

☐ Plan a budget for your Patrol or unit, covering things like badges, rent, equipment, magazines, outings and anything else your Patrol/unit has planned for a term.

☐ Find out how much telephone calls to different places cost.

☐ Make cakes and raise money with a cake sale.

☐ Plan a fundraising campaign

to buy a piece of equipment for your unit – perhaps a lightweight tent or a tape recorder, or anything you need. Raise the money, look at different tents (or whatever), decide what you want – and buy!

☐ Look at your unit accounts to see what your money is spent on. What sort of account is it? How many signatories are needed?

☐ Collect symbols and logos of different banks, building societies, etc and look at them. What do the logos tell you about how the organizations want people to think about them?

☐ Find out the differences between cash, cheques, direct debit cards, credit cards and hire purchase. Do a survey to find out which people prefer and why.

☐ Find out how to open a bank account and how cheques and bank cards are used. How old do you have to be before you can open an account or hold a cheque, credit or debit card?

☐ Find out about the currencies of other countries. If you go abroad for your holidays compare the price of goods like records, trainers and T-shirts from some other countries.

□ Your Patrol has £5 to feed a family of four for supper. Visit shops and the supermarket and find out prices – what would you cook to produce a healthy balanced meal? Why not prepare the meal for someone?

□ Invite an accountant or someone who works in a bank to come to a Company meeting and explain what they do.

YOU ARE A CONSUMER

Taking decisions about what to buy makes you a consumer, but do you know what went into making that decision?

IDEAS

□ Collect advertisements from magazines and newspapers and discuss which are the most appealing and why. Have you ever bought anything just because of a good advertisement?

□ Compare different television advertisements. How much time does each channel devote to advertising? Which are the most effective advertisements and why? See if you can spot advertising within television programmes as well. Discuss your reactions with others and decide what the arguments for and against television

advertising are.

□ Find out about your rights as a consumer. Can you take clothes back to the shop and ask for your money back or do you have to accept a credit note? Does it make a difference to your rights if you buy something in the sales? Your local Citizens' Advice Bureau or Town Hall should be able to help.

USEFUL SKILLS

Are you a useful person to have around? Could you wire a plug? Telephone for an ambulance? Keep calm in a fire? Defrost the freezer? Mend a bicycle puncture? Turn off the water, gas or electricity? Saw a piece of wood and use an electric drill?

Make yourself useful and learn skills whenever you get the chance – you never know when you might need them!

Make an emergency telephone call

There are various different kinds of telephones nowadays, but the basics are …
● Dial 999 (you don't need money or a card).
● When the operator answers, say which service you require: Fire, Police, Ambulance,

Coastguard or Mountain/Cave Rescue.
● Give the telephone number shown on the phone (or its location if there is no number).
● When the service answers, give the following information: The address or location where help is needed, e.g. 'Ambulance to 14 Long Street, East Town', or 'Car crash at the junction of Front Street and Main Road, Castletown,' other details, like 'four people injured' or 'chemical lorry involved'.

In case of fire remember the three 'outs':
Get out
get the fire brigade out
stay out!

EMERGENCY DRILL

You've probably had a fire drill at school – an alarm sounds and everyone leaves the building as quickly as they can and meets in a safe place, where a register is called to ensure no one has been left behind.

Have an emergency drill at your meeting place. Talk to your Guiders and, if you all think it would be safe, you could try holding one without warning. Then talk in Patrols about how it went and how things could be improved. Each Patrol could write instructions for a fire drill and then a small group could write one for the whole unit including all the best ideas.

In an emergency at home (for example a fire), how would you get out? Work out how you and your family would get to safety if there was a fire in your kitchen or another part of the house.

WIRING A PLUG

Use a small screwdriver and be careful not to lose the small screws when loosened. Remember the green-and-yellow wires should be attached to the Earth terminal, blue is Neutral and brown is Live. Make sure you use the correct fuse.

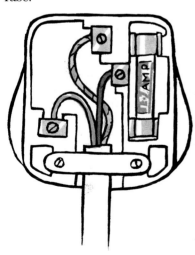

DEFROST THE FREEZER

Some freezers defrost themselves but not all! The best time to defrost the freezer is when there is very little food being stored in it – the less food you have to keep frozen while you're defrosting, the better!

Empty the freezer and put frozen food somewhere it will not defrost (for example next door's freezer, or in a coolbox, wrapped in newspaper with a freezerpack). It's very important that the food doesn't defrost while it's out of the freezer.

Turn off the power at the wall switch. Open the freezer door. If the freezer has a drain at the bottom, position a bowl under it.

You can put a cloth on the freezer floor to absorb melting ice, and place a bowl of hot water on the bottom shelf to help raise the temperature.

When all the ice has melted, pour the water away and wipe the sides, shelf and door down with fridge cleaner or a solution of bicarbonate of soda in warm water.

Close the door and turn the power back on. Put the frozen food (still frozen!) back into the freezer.

SAW WOOD/USE A DRILL/ SCREWDRIVER/HAMMER

The important thing about do-it-yourself is to use the right tool for the job – it's safer and you'll do a better job.

or turn the wood over and saw gently from the other side to prevent the wood splitting

When sawing wood:
– mark where you want to cut

Using a drill

– hold the wood steady (use a vice if necessary)
– draw the saw across the wood to make a dent
– saw backwards and forwards with a rhythm
– when you're nearly through, go more gently,

– mark the spot
– hold the drill steady
– apply an even pressure

Using a hammer

– mark the spot
– hold the nail between thumb and finger
– tap gently until the wood holds the nail, then let go
– carry on hammering gently until the nail is flush with the wood

TURN OFF WATER/GAS/ELECTRICITY/READ METER

Most people have mains services to their homes – electricity, water and sometimes gas. Although we're so used to having them available, they can all be dangerous if not treated with respect, so learn to live with them now!

In some emergencies such as an electric shock, gas leak or burst water pipe, you'll need to be able to turn off any of the services at the mains, that is, where they come into the house.

In your house, look for
- the mains electricity switch
- the mains water tap (it may be outside)
- the gas tap (if you use gas)

Find out how to turn them off in an emergency.
Often the main gas or electricity tap or switch is beside the meter, so find out how to read the meters in your house, too!

If anyone you know has a water meter, find out from them how it works.

MEND A PUNCTURE

No matter how careful you are with your bike, you'll probably get a puncture one day, so it's good to know how to deal with it.

First turn your bike upside down so it stands on the saddle and handlebars. Check the valve carefully as this may be where the leak is. If tightening or replacing the valve does not

solve the problem then deflate the tyre and use two tyre levers to remove the tyre and inner tube (be careful not to damage the inner tube).

Carefully look along the inner tube for the puncture.
Find tiny holes

with a bowl of water: hold the tube underwater a section at a time. A thread of bubbles will rise as air in the tube escapes from the hole.

Dry the tube and dust with chalk. Cut a patch to cover the hole and stick down over the hole using rubber adhesive.

Fit the tube inside the tyre, lining up the valve with the opening in the tyre. Carefully lever the tyre and tube back on to the wheel. Inflate the tyre until it is board hard.

Now you can change a bicycle tyre ... find out how to change a car wheel!

IDEAS

♣ Make a toy or game out of wood.

♣ Learn how to unblock a sink or drain. What protection should you wear?

♣ Look after your bike. Learn how to mend a puncture, replace a chain and look after your lights.

☐ Change the gas cylinder in a portable stove. Practise by re-inserting an empty cylinder to start with. Ask an adult to help first time.

♣ Know where the mains switches for gas, water and electricity services turn on and off for your home or meeting place.

♣ Learn how to read the gas and electricity meters.

☐ Know how to wire a plug and change fuses.

☐ Clean and paint an old chair, a door or a windowsill. (Ask your parents first!)

☐ Find out how the overflow system on the toilet works. Show your Patrol.

♣ Dripping taps waste water! Find out how to stop a tap dripping.

☐ Visit your local DIY store and find out about the different types of wood they sell.

'God has given us a world to live in that is full of beauties and wonders and he has given us not only eyes to see them but minds to understand them, if only we have the sense to look at them in that light.'

**B-P's LAST MESSAGE
TO GIRL GUIDES**

4

Guides should get into the out-of-doors as often as they can — it has one of the Eight Points all to itself and it can come into all the others, too! Even if you meet in an area where you can't spend time outside during your meetings, you can still try to get out for Patrol meetings and weekend trips.

Whatever you are going to do outdoors it makes sense to:

- plan ahead
- dress correctly
- be safe
- protect the environment
- know what you're doing.

PLANNING AHEAD

Don't forget the skills you use when you're planning Patrol activities. Think about:
- **what to do, where to go, when to go**
- **whether you need practice before you go**
- **what to wear**
- **where to get equipment and food, and who will bring it**
- **special safety needs (whether you need a leader; emergency phone numbers, etc) Make a list of who is responsible for what. (see page 89)**
- **make sure you tell your parents where you are going and get their permission first.**

DRESSING CORRECTLY

For most outdoor activities you are best in trousers or shorts, a shirt or t-shirt and a jumper or sweatshirt, with boots, trainers or wellingtons on your feet. This can vary according to the weather and what you're doing, as some activities are actually dangerous if you are not dressed properly. On pages with activities on them you will find pictures of Guides dressed properly for them.

BEING SAFE

Each activity has its own special safety rules which every member of the group should know and follow. Most of them are common sense – like not

going hiking on your own, or being able to swim if you want to go canoeing, or wearing a helmet for abseiling. You will find safety information on the activity pages, but don't forget your personal safety code on page 53.

PROTECTING THE ENVIRONMENT

We have been given the land to look after. Future generations depend on us to preserve the environment for them. Guides all over the world care about this. Remember the Country Code when you are anywhere out of doors – most of it applies just as much to the town!

THE COUNTRY CODE

1 Enjoy the countryside and respect its life and work

2 Guard against all risk of fire

3 Fasten all gates

4 Keep your dogs under close control

5 Keep to public paths across farmland

6 Use gates and stiles to cross fences, hedges and walls

7 Leave livestock, crops and machinery alone

8 Take your litter home

9 Help to keep all water clean

10 Protect wildlife, plants and trees

11 Take special care on country roads

12 Make no unnecessary noise

KNOW WHAT YOU ARE DOING

You'll be able to enjoy the out-of-doors much more if you know what you are doing – that is, if you have some skills or knowledge. Sometimes you will do a lot of preparation before an activity, while other times you will be 'learning by doing'. Some of the basic things every Guide should know include:

- **using map and compass to find her way**
- **lighting a fire and cooking a meal**
- **recognizing changes in weather conditions**
- **taking notice of nature**
- **caring for the environment**
- **using knots**

All these are skills which will help you to have fun doing activities like pioneering, hiking, tracking or cooking in the out-of-doors. This chapter will help you with some of them.

OUTDOOR KNOW-HOW
FIRES AND FOOD

Whether it's a backyard barbecue or a lifesaving exercise, cooking out of doors is a great way to learn a useful skill while having fun.

For a Patrol cook-out, you will need:
- a safe place to build a fire or stand a camping stove or barbecue
- fuel for the fire or stove
- food and some way of preparing it
- a bin liner or bag for rubbish

MAKING A FIRE

Fires need three things: fuel, oxygen and heat.

First collect your fuel – an ordinary fire at camp will need a large pile of burnable wood to cook a small meal for an average-sized Patrol. So keep people wooding, even when you've got the fire going!

You'll need three types of wood:

Punk to catch the flame – dry leaves (holly or sweet chestnut are best), dead gorse; dry bark from dead trees; dead bramble; wood shavings; pine needles, pine cones.

Kindling to get the fire going – twigs (no thicker than a match) of holly, birch, beech, larch, hawthorn, ash.

PUNK   KINDLING

Fuel to burn and create heat for cooking – thicker pieces of wood from beech, ash, oak, holly, hawthorn, birch.
Never cut wood from living trees – there's usually no need, as dead wood can be found on the ground. You should only burn dead wood (most live or green wood doesn't burn very well, anyway).

1 Make a fireplace
2 Place punk in centre of fireplace.
3 Add kindling, loosely, either in a pyramid or in a 'cobhouse'. Have slightly larger twigs ready to add quickly.
4 Light the match with its head down and sheltered. Light the punk on the side the wind is blowing from. (This provides the heat!)

BRICK FIREPLACE

5 Add thicker wood until a good fire gets going. Don't swamp the fire – give it air. Fan the flames with a metal plate if you need to.
6 Be safe – have a bucket of water or pile of earth or sand ready to put the fire out quickly if you need to. (These work by taking away the fire's oxygen supply.)

Tips for successful firelighting
• Collect plenty of wood before lighting a fire.
• Break it up into handy sizes and make a woodpile nearby

WOOD PILE

• Glowing embers cook things much better than flames.
• Clear up with care. Let the fire die down, then add water, slowly. When cold, dig the ashes into the earth, or dispose of them in a suitable place, such as a muddy corner or pathway.
• Make sure your fire is really out – in some places the heat can spread underground and cause a fire somewhere else after you have gone.

Don't scorch the grass — use a pan rest

WHAT TO COOK

♣ Start with something simple such as toasted marshmallows or twists (Mix a cup of self-raising flour with enough water to make a stiff dough, twist lengths of dough round a green stick each and cook over the fire).

♣ Try foil cooking. Wrap up cheese sandwiches, with the margarine or butter on the outside or wrap up bananas sprinkled with lemon juice and brown sugar. Or slit bananas

lengthways and stick in three squares of chocolate before wrapping in foil. Leave to cook for 5–10 minutes. Don't forget to take your foil home with you!

♣ Boiling water can be used for many different things: hot cocoa, soup, instant rice, boiled eggs, pasta and vegetables.

♣ One pot meals are easy to make and clean up after. Cook savoury mince and pasta and rice with tinned tomatoes, onions and other vegetables. Beanfeast meals are simple and tasty. If you make a stew, cut the potatoes into small pieces and cook them in the gravy.

♣ Experiment – produce Patrol specialities ready for camp!

Try some of the recipes in the next chapter on camp, page 119.

WHAT TO

COOK

FINDING THE WAY
MAP AND COMPASS

Using a map is a very useful skill in town or country. There are different types and sizes of maps – for example:

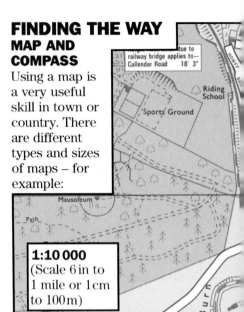

1:10 000
(Scale 6 in to 1 mile or 1 cm to 100m)

© Crown Copyright

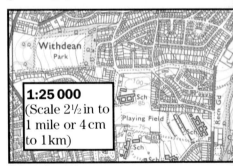

1:25 000
(Scale 2½ in to 1 mile or 4 cm to 1 km)

© Crown Copyright

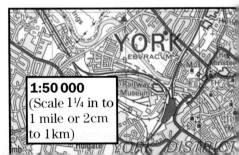

1:50 000
(Scale 1¼ in to 1 mile or 2 cm to 1 km)

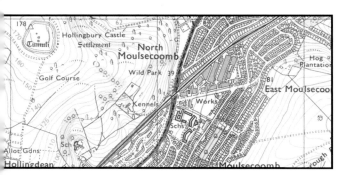

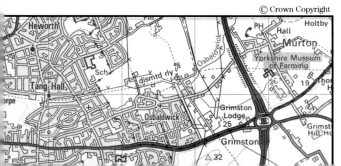

© Crown Copyright

USING A STREET MAP

Most cities and towns have a street map – a bird's eye view of the layout of the streets and roads in them. They have an index so that you can find the street or road you want: the map key (or legend) to find out how different types of road are shown on the map you are using, as this varies from map to map.

☐ Using a road map, with your Patrol find symbols for: challenge for another Patrol.

USING AN ORDNANCE SURVEY MAP (1:25 000)

The next page shows an extract from a 1:25 000 Ordnance Survey map, and you will

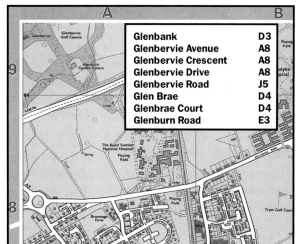

Glenbank	D3
Glenbervie Avenue	A8
Glenbervie Crescent	A8
Glenbervie Drive	A8
Glenbervie Road	J5
Glen Brae	D4
Glenbrae Court	D4
Glenburn Road	E3

© Crown Copyright

USING A ROAD MAP

If you travel in a car a lot it's useful to know how to read a road map. Use motorway service areas; castles; lighthouses; railway lines; picnic areas. Make up a find a key showing symbols for some of the things you would find in the area shown.

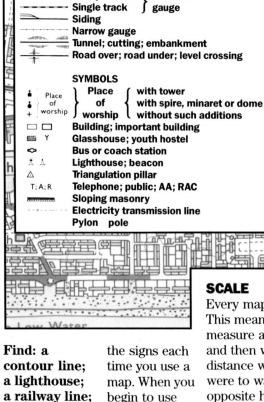

© Crown Copyright

RAILWAYS
——— Multiple track } Standard
——— Single track } gauge
——— Siding
——— Narrow gauge
——— Tunnel; cutting; embankment
——— Road over; road under; level crossing

SYMBOLS
Place of worship } Place of worship { with tower
with spire, minaret or dome
without such additions
Building; important building
Glasshouse; youth hostel
Bus or coach station
Lighthouse; beacon
Triangulation pillar
Telephone; public; AA; RAC
Sloping masonry
Electricity transmission line
Pylon   pole

Find: a contour line; a lighthouse; a railway line; a place of worship.

A complete list of the symbols is printed on each OS map. This is called the legend. Try to learn more of the signs each time you use a map. When you begin to use different maps you will find that sometimes colours or symbols are different, so always check the legend if you're not sure.

SCALE

Every map is drawn to a scale. This means that you can measure a distance on the map and then work out how far the distance would really be if you were to walk it. The map opposite has a scale of 1:25 000. This means that every 1cm on the map equals 25,000cm (250m) on the ground. From this you can work out that 4cm equals 1km on the ground. A map with a scale of 1:10 000 shows a smaller area of ground in more detail.

☐ Borrow different maps of the same area and compare them. Which are easier to read? Which are more useful?

CONTOUR LINES

Contour lines indicate the height and steepness of the land. Find a contour line on the map above and follow it. A number on a contour line gives the height of the land in metres above sea level (or feet, if you have an old map – check which!). The legend on the map tells you the height between the contour lines – the contour interval. If the interval is 10m,

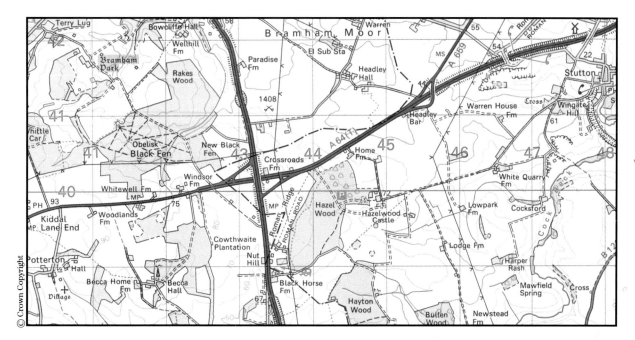

© Crown Copyright

the next brown line will be 10m higher or lower. When contour lines are close together you know the hill is steep. If they are far apart, expect a gentle slope.

☐ Make a sketch map of your area. Make sure that North is at the top of your map and include a legend. Work out a way of giving your map a scale.

GRID REFERENCES

OS maps are all based on the National Grid reference system. This system divides up the country into 100 km squares and each square is given two grid letters.

These large squares are divided into smaller 1 km squares. These are the squares printed on OS maps.

To find a grid reference:
You need to know the grid reference for the church in Stutton. This is given in six figures. The 'easting' or vertical line is numbered 47. Now imagine the side of the square is divided into ten equal parts. The church is nine-tenths across the square so the first three figures are 479. Now do the same for the 'northings' or horizontal lines. The first figures will be 41. The church is five-tenths of the way up the square so the third figure is 5. This gives the full six-figure grid reference for the church as 479 415.

Remember which number comes first by thinking 'Along the corridor and up the stairs' or 'crawl before you walk'.

Sometimes you will need to use a zero to complete a grid

reference. Give the grid references for one of the farms shown on the map.

SETTING A MAP

A map is no good unless you can use it to find your way! *Set your map* by turning it (and yourself) so that the symbols on the map line up with the actual features on the ground.

Find two or more landmarks and line them up with their symbols on the map. Check using other landmarks, and then the map is set.

You can do this with any map before you use it.

USING A COMPASS

When there are lots of things to set your map by, you will be able to follow it without a compass – but it's not always that easy! If you're lost, or the weather is bad and you can't see far ahead, or if you're orienteering, you'll need to be able to use a compass.

To find your way, you need to know where north is – but as there are three 'norths', that's not as easy as it sounds!

Magnetic north – near the North Pole, nearly at the top of the world, there is an area of magnetic rock. This is the north your compass needle will point to.

Grid north – the 'eastings' on your map, going from top to bottom, point towards Grid north at the top of the map.

True north – is the direction of the North Pole.

Grid north and True north are not exactly the same but are close enough for map-reading in the UK. The difference between true north and magnetic north varies from year to year, and you have to work this out every time (see below).

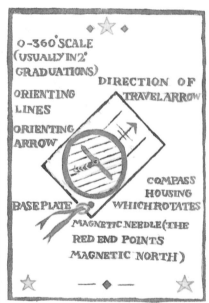

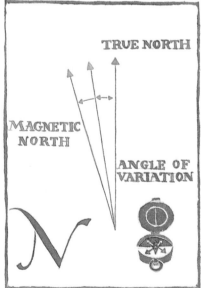

TRUE NORTH

MAGNETIC NORTH

ANGLE OF VARIATION

SETTING YOUR COMPASS

1. Hold the compass flat and turn the housing until 'N' is next to the 'direction of travel' arrow.

2. Turn yourself around until the red end of the needle lines up with the orienting arrow.

3. You are now facing towards magnetic north.

BEARINGS

Put simply, bearings are directions. You probably know 16 points of the compass – perhaps more – but by using bearings we can have 360, which means we can be much more accurate.

The compass dial is marked to show 360° degrees, and each small mark around the dial stands for two degrees.

Due West = 270°
Due East = 90°
Due South =
Due North =
South-west =
North-east =
East-south-east =

☐ Challenge each other to convert compass points into bearings.

WALKING ON A BEARING

Suppose you have to walk on a bearing of 82°.

1. Turn the housing so that 82° lines up with the direction of travel arrow.

2. Holding the compass flat in your hand, turn yourself until the red end of the needle lines up with the orienting arrow and points to the N on the housing.

3. Keeping the needle over the orienting arrow, look along the direction of travel arrow and pick an object (a tree, a rock, a tower, etc) in that direction.

4. Walk towards the object you have chosen, stopping every now and again to check you are still following your bearing.

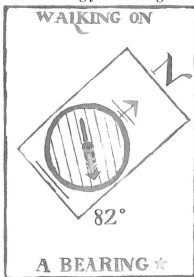

WALKING ON

82°

A BEARING ☆

☐ Compass Sculpture.

'Draw' a shape on the ground using string and walking on different bearings.

Mark the start with a peg knocked into the ground and walk on the first bearing. Put in another peg and join the two with string. Repeat for all the other bearings, using the string stretched between pages to make a shape:

Walk for 3 metres on a bearing of 010°. Put in a peg.

3 metres	154°
3 metres	298°
3 metres	082°
3 metres	226°

What shape do you now have? (Your shape should look like a star – if not, try again!)

☐ Work out the bearings and distances for other shapes –

squares, triangles, hexagons, a house with a chimney, and challenge other Patrols.

☐ Practise taking bearings.

Go outside and take compass bearings for buildings, trees, hills, bus stops, etc.

1 Holding the compass flat, point the direction of travel arrow at your landmark.
2 Keeping the arrow pointed at the object, turn the compass housing until the red end of the needle lines up over the orienting arrow.
3 Read the bearing of the landmark at the bottom of the direction of travel arrow.

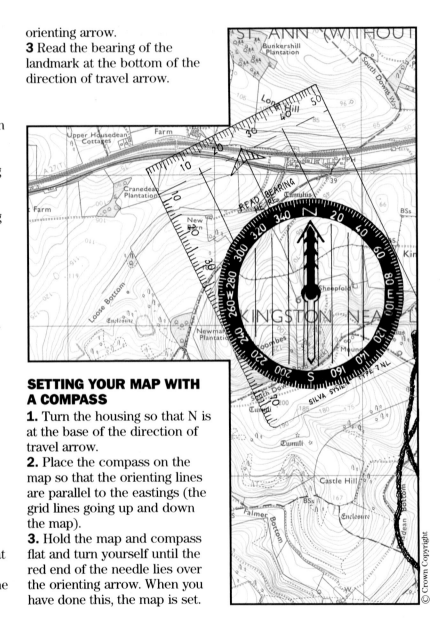

© Crown Copyright

SETTING YOUR MAP WITH A COMPASS

1. Turn the housing so that N is at the base of the direction of travel arrow.
2. Place the compass on the map so that the orienting lines are parallel to the eastings (the grid lines going up and down the map).
3. Hold the map and compass flat and turn yourself until the red end of the needle lies over the orienting arrow. When you have done this, the map is set.

To be even more accurate, make allowance for **magnetic variation**, which is the difference between true north and magnetic north, where the needle is pointing. In the UK, the magnetic variation is between 5° and 6.5° west of true North depending on where you live – look at the margin of your map for details.

ALLOWING FOR MAGNETIC VARIATION

You can do this when you have set your map. Subtract the magnetic variation from 360° and, holding the compass in place, turn the housing gently so the new number lines up with the base of the direction of travel arrow.

So, if the magnetic variation is 6° W, you turn the compass so that the needle points to 354°:

$$360° - 6° = 354°.$$

When you are planning a hike, you usually break your journey up into small stages. For each stage you can use a bearing to make sure you are walking in the right direction. You can use grid bearings or you can be more accurate and use magnetic bearings, which take account of the difference between true and magnetic north.

GRID BEARINGS

Suppose you want to get from Lodge Farm at 457 393 (A) to the Public House in Towton at 484 396 (B) by walking on a bearing:

1. Place the compass flat on your map with the base plate lined up against A and B. Make sure the direction of travel arrow points the way you want to go!

2. Turn the compass housing until the orienting lines are parallel with the grid lines of the map (ignore the needle as it swings). The 'N' on the dial should point towards the top of the map.

3. Remove the compass and read the bearing shown at the base of the direction of travel arrow.

MAGNETIC BEARINGS

For more accuracy, you should add the magnetic variation to your grid bearing.

So, if the grid bearing is 82°, you should add the magnetic variation (work out what it is from the information on the map) to 82°, and move the housing gently round so that the new number is at the base of the direction of travel arrow.

Turn the whole compass until the red end of the needle points to 'N' on the dial. The 'direction of travel' arrow is now pointing in exactly the right direction.

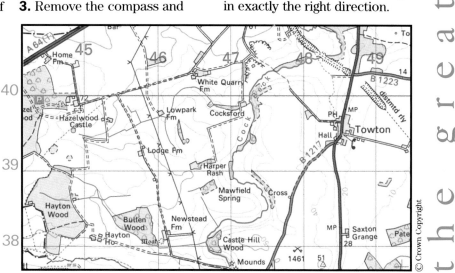

the great outdoors

DIRECTIONS IN THE SKY

If you don't have a compass you can still find north quite accurately by using the sun by day and stars by night.

USING THE SUN

You will need a watch face with hands for this (if you have a digital watch, draw a clock face showing the correct time). Hold the watch flat and point the hour hand to the sun. South lies half-way between the hour hand and noon (12 o'clock in winter, but 1 o'clock during British Summer Time). North, of course, is in the opposite direction.

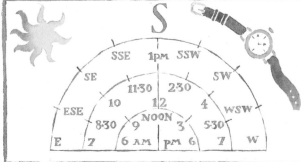

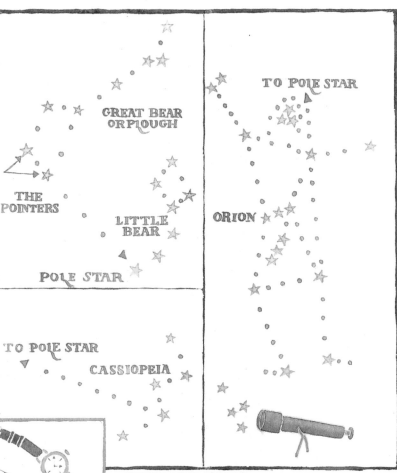

GREAT BEAR OR PLOUGH

THE POINTERS

LITTLE BEAR

POLE STAR

TO POLE STAR

ORION

TO POLE STAR

CASSIOPEIA

USING THE STARS

Use the constellations to help you find the Pole (or North) star.

COMMUNICATION
SEMAPHORE

Use flags or just your arms to send messages when you can't hear but you can see the person you're communicating with! Each letter of the alphabet is represented by a different position.

☐ Spell out your name, Patrol and unit.

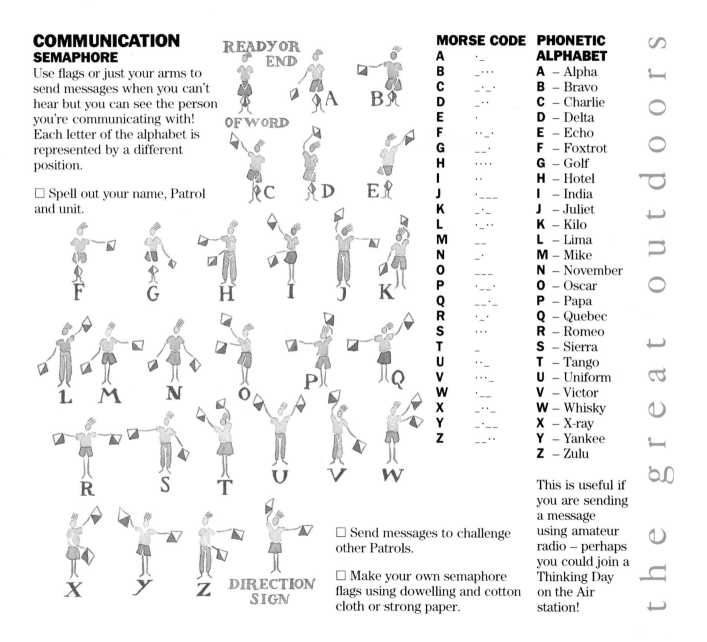

READY OR END OF WORD

A B C D E

F G H I J K

L M N O P Q

R S T U V W

X Y Z DIRECTION SIGN

MORSE CODE		PHONETIC ALPHABET
A	·_	A – Alpha
B	_···	B – Bravo
C	_·_·	C – Charlie
D	_··	D – Delta
E	·	E – Echo
F	··_·	F – Foxtrot
G	__·	G – Golf
H	····	H – Hotel
I	··	I – India
J	·___	J – Juliet
K	_·_	K – Kilo
L	·_··	L – Lima
M	__	M – Mike
N	_·	N – November
O	___	O – Oscar
P	·__·	P – Papa
Q	__·_	Q – Quebec
R	·_·	R – Romeo
S	···	S – Sierra
T	_	T – Tango
U	··_	U – Uniform
V	···_	V – Victor
W	·__	W – Whisky
X	_··_	X – X-ray
Y	_·__	Y – Yankee
Z	__··	Z – Zulu

☐ Send messages to challenge other Patrols.

☐ Make your own semaphore flags using dowelling and cotton cloth or strong paper.

This is useful if you are sending a message using amateur radio – perhaps you could join a Thinking Day on the Air station!

the great outdoors

HAND AND WHISTLE SIGNALS

Knowing hand and whistle signals is especially useful at camp or when you are working in large open spaces.

Whistle Signals

– = short blast   ___ = long blast

1	–	'Attention'
2	___	'Silence' or 'Halt'
3	– – –	'Come here'
4	___ ___ ___	'Go further out' or 'Scatter'
5	– ___ – ___	'Warning' or 'Be ready'
6	– – – ___	'Leaders come here'

And, of course: – – – – – ___ ___ – – – – – ___ !

Hand Signals

SILENCE & LISTEN   HALT

COME HERE QUICKLY   GO FURTHER OUT OR SCATTER

SIT   AS YOU WERE.

WEATHER

Weather is important for life – as well as needing a balance of sun and rain to ripen crops, people want good weather for camp, holidays or weddings, or snow for Christmas, or even plenty of wind for sailing or flying kites! When you go on more adventurous activities, what the weather does becomes much more important. Weather conditions can change very rapidly so you need to know how to spot the signs for change.

If you watch a television weather forecast you'll notice that our weather almost always moves from left to right, or from west to east. Our weather usually comes in from the Atlantic Ocean – sometimes we get the remains of tropical storms from the West Indies – and then the weather moves away again across Europe, either northwards to Scandinavia and the USSR or southwards to France and Spain. Watch as the presenter 'runs the sequence' to show how the weather is moving across the British Isles.

Before you go on an activity find out about the weather forecast. Is the weather going to change later in the day? Is rain

the great outdoors

expected? Will you need to take sunscreen cream? Be Prepared for the weather conditions.

Sometimes the weather can change faster than the forecast. If you can read the weather, so that you can see changes coming, you'll be able to make plans. So keep an eye on the sky and know what the signs mean.

CLOUDS

In winter when you breathe out your moist breath hits cold air and forms a little 'cloud'. Clouds in the sky are formed in the same way. When water vapour in the atmosphere cools, it condenses around tiny bits of dust and salt in the air and makes clouds.

Different shapes of clouds mean different types of weather is coming. Look out for these types of cloud and record what sort of weather followed them over the next day or so:

Stratocumulus (Sc)

Cumulonimbus (Cb)

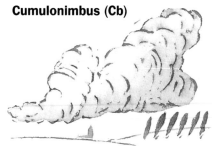

Nimbostratus (Nb)

Cirrus (Ci)

The descriptions of clouds come from Latin words:

Cumulus – indicates hot air rising
Nimbus – means raining or snowing
Cirrus – wispy threads
Stratus – layers
Alto – high up

The colour of the sky can tell you about the weather too. You probably know the old saying:

> Red sky at night,
> shepherd's delight.
> Red sky in the morning,
> shepherd's warning

but have you ever watched the weather to see if it is true?

☐ Collect weather sayings and see how true they are.
☐ Gliders and birds use hot air to rise high in the air. Make paper aeroplanes and see how you can make them fly using hot air currents (such as hair dryers, toasters, radiators, etc. Take care you don't set your aeroplanes alight!)

WIND

Do you know how to tell which way the wind is blowing? Just wet a finger and hold it in the air – the side which gets cold first is the side the wind is blowing from.

Wind is what happens when air moves. When the air gets hot, it rises, and is replaced by cooler air, which in turn gets warm and rises, so you can see the air is moving all the time.

Although most of our weather comes from the south-west, the wind can come from any direction – especially around our coasts – and a change in the wind direction often means a change in the weather is coming.

There is a scale to help people to estimate the wind speed by watching what effect it has on the environment. It is known as the **Beaufort Scale**.

Force Number	Description of wind
0	calm
1	light air
2	light breeze
3	gentle breeze
4	moderate breeze
5	fresh breeze
6	strong breeze
7	moderate gale
8	fresh gale
9	strong gale
10	whole gale
11	storm
12	hurricane

♣ Make a rain gauge

MAKE A RAIN GAUGE

TOP MUST BE 30 cm ABOVE EARTH SO PLACE IN HOLE IN GROUND IF NECESSARY

←DCM→

SHARP EDGE

DIAMETER ABOUT 12·5 cm

ABOUT 15 CM HIGH

FUNNEL WITH TIN EXTENSION SOLDERED ON

SOLDER OR WAX.

COLLECTING VESSEL — STRAIGHT SIDES AND FLAT BASE

Stand your rain gauge in the open – not too close to buildings which might shelter it or trees which might drip into it. Don't expect to collect gallons of water!

☐ Keep a thermometer on the shady side of your house to record the air temperature. Try to look at it at the same times every day. If you have a minimum/maximum thermometer you can record the warmest and coolest times of the day.

☐ At camp set up a Patrol weather station – make records of the weather at the end of every day and try to forecast what the next day will be like.

☐ If each member of the Patrol makes the same equipment, you could set up smaller weather stations at everyone's home and see if there is any difference in the weather around your homes.

☐ Some schools have weather recording equipment – find out how to use it and help keep the records for a while.

☐ Find out what the weather charts in the newspaper and on television mean.

☐ Make a weather vane

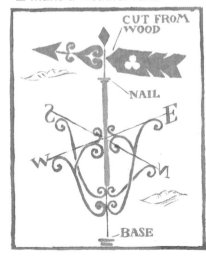

CUT FROM WOOD

NAIL

E

W

BASE

The arrow should balance and swing freely on the nail – oil it if necessary.

KNOTS

Guides have a reputation for being able to tie knots — and there are all sorts of occasions when they can come in handy. Here are some of the most common and what they are used for:

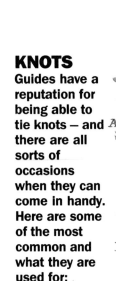

DOUBLE OVERHAND

REEF

CLOVE HITCH

BOWLINE

BOWLINE ON A BIGHT

ROUND TURN AND TWO HALF HITCHES

SHEET BEND

LARKS HEAD

WESTCOUNTRYWHIPPING

REEF KNOT

→ = PULL

Double overhand – to keep ropes tidy, to tie up guy lines at camp and to make a loop.

Reef – to join two ropes of the same thickness or to fasten a bandage.

Clove hitch – to fasten one end of a rope to a tree or post, or a toggle to a flag.

Sheepshank – to shorten a rope.

Bowline – to make a loop that won't slip.

Bowline on a bight – a good rescue knot.

Round turn and two half hitches – for tying up any moving object like a boat or an animal. Also for attaching a rope to a bar or ring.

Sheet bend – for joining a thin rope to a thicker rope, e.g. when attaching a flag to a halyard.

Lark's head – to loop a rope around a ring.

West Country whipping – a simple way to tidy up a frayed rope end (More knots on page 81.)

When you're learning knots don't mess around with bits of string – invest in some thin rope for your Patrol box and use that! Practise tying knots behind your back and in the dark so that you can do it almost without thinking – but remember, it's no use learning knots if you never use them again!

Have fun and practise knots with some of these activities

the great outdoors

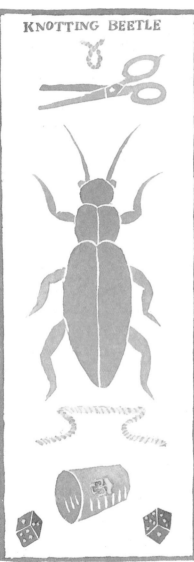

KNOTTING BEETLE

Make heads and bodies from card. Use a punch to make holes.

☐ Knotting Beetle

Cut string – 12 × 15cm per player
You need a dice and a shaker

Take turns throwing the dice. You need a six to get the body and a five for the head. Win other parts of the beetle's body by throwing:

1 = tail – tie it on using a bowline
2 = legs (6) – round turn and two half hitches
3 = antennae (2) – sheet bend
4 = mandibles (2) lark's head
5 = neck (tie head to body) = reef knot
6 = any part you haven't got

Collect one piece at a time – not all six legs in one go!

☐ Blindfold knotting

Use a clean blindfold for each player and don't leave them on for more than 10 minutes.

Patrol Leader calls out a knot; Guides tie it

Patrol Leader gives each member of the Patrol a knot already tied to identify by touch. Have several different knots for everyone to feel

Same again, only this time all the Guides have the same knot – first to untie it and call out its name wins.

☐ The chain

Guides stand in a circle, each with a length of rope. When someone calls out 'go', everyone must try to tie a clove hitch round the leg of the person on their right while trying to stop the person on their left tying a clove hitch round their leg. Repeat tying other knots (e.g. round turn and two half-hitches, bowline, etc).

THE CHAIN

☐ Knot challenge

Make up situations for other Patrols to act out using the right knots. For example: You are at camp when suddenly you find a goat in the store tent. Take it back to the farmer using the right knots.

☐ Knotting pairs

In pairs, tie knots using right hands only. Repeat using left hands only.

☐ Macramé

Decorative knots. Borrow a book from the library and amaze your friends. Or make a Turk's Head woggle!

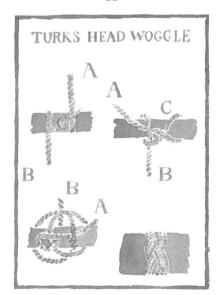

TURKS HEAD WOGGLE

ENJOYING THE OUT-OF-DOORS
TRACKING AND TRAILING

Following a trail is a good way of seeing how observant you are. Make tracking signs using natural materials or draw them in chalk.

Make a trail of objects – use feathers, rice, nuts, even wool, or paper, as long as whoever is following picks it all up afterwards. Try a sniffing trail – rub half a lemon on lamp posts, walls, etc, for a town trail with a difference!

Another way of tracking is to follow the trails animals leave behind them without knowing it – footprints, pawprints, droppings, damaged vegetation and bits of fur or hair.

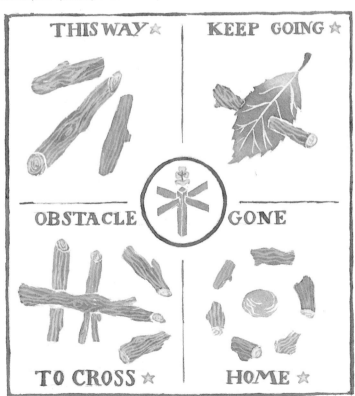

THIS WAY ☆   KEEP GOING ☆

OBSTACLE   GONE

TO CROSS ☆   HOME ☆

RABBIT

SQUIRREL

BADGER

RAT

HEDGEHOG

FOX

☐ In your Patrol, find a stretch of sand or smooth soil and practise making tracks and working out which is which. Try walking, running, tiptoeing, taking extra-big steps, etc. Measure the different lengths of paces. Could you use your pace to estimate distances?

☐ Look for animal tracks where you live. Animals leave the best tracks in soft, muddy ground or snow. Badgers, squirrels and foxes all visit gardens in built up areas to look for food.

☐ Why not try preserving an animal's track by making a plaster cast?

☐ Have a Patrol guessing game to decide whose hand or foot prints are whose. Using poster paint everyone makes their track across a large piece of paper. What are the differences? If you mix them up do you know whose is whose?

STALKING

If you're a naturalist, you'll know how important it is to be able to stay still and silent when you're watching an animal or bird. If you're really quiet, you can actually follow creatures without them paying too much attention to you. You can use these stalking techniques in games at Guides, too – if you have a safe area where you can play stalking games it can be a lot of fun!

Stalking successfully:

● **Keep quiet and move slowly.** Even if you are seen, you might not be noticed.

● **Use cover** – hedges, walls, shadows, trees etc so that you don't stand out like a sore thumb.

● If you're watching animals and birds, **clothes in natural colours** – greens and browns – **help to camouflage you.** (If you're out on the hills, though, it's sometimes better to have **bright colours** so that you can be seen if you ever need to be rescued).

● **Don't stand out against the horizon** – keep low and away from hilltops.

● **Wear quiet clothes and shoes.** Don't tread on twigs or small stones.

● **Stay downwind of animals** – they can smell your scent on the wind.

● **Walk slowly, crouch and walk**, crawl on hands and knees or even work your way along on your stomach, depending on which is best for the creature you're stalking.

KEYS

(Practically every Guide Company has its own version of this game!) Everyone sits in a circle, with one person in the middle, blindfolded with a bunch of keys in front of her. Someone points to different girls, who stand up and walk right round the inside of the circle before trying to pick up the keys in front of the listener. If the listener hears a sound she can point at the walker or try to grab her. If the walker gets the keys she becomes the listener.

FUN OUT-OF-DOORS

☐ **Follow a trail in a built-up area.** Use whatever you like: windows, roofs, chimneys, pillar boxes and other street furniture.

☐ **Lay a compass trail.**

☐ **Go on a penny hike** – every time you come to a junction, flip a coin: heads – turn right, tails – turn left.

☐ **Make your Patrol emblem** out of natural materials and cover it with transparent sticky-backed plastic to keep it safe.

☐ **Make and fly a glider** or a kite.

☐ **Make a spider's web and spider** (using straws, black thread and black pipe cleaners).

☐ **Make leaf prints** – carbon ones. Layer a piece of white paper over a leaf, over a sheet of carbon paper, over another piece of white paper. Iron the top sheet.

☐ **Cook pancakes on top of a tin can.** Or make a buddy burner and cook them over that.

☐ **A unit activity** – each Patrol makes up a rhyming treasure hunt for another Patrol to follow.

● **Stargazing** – create a planetarium (place for looking at the stars) using an old black or dark blue umbrella. Stick on paper constellations (groups of stars) and planets as they appear in the sky. You can use a large sheet of black or dark blue card if you haven't an umbrella.

□ **Create animal models** using stones and glue. Add a finishing touch with gloss or enamel paint.

□ **Build an igloo, wigwam, natural shelter or a 'hide'** for watching animals or birds. Make a Patrol den.

□ **Be a Backwoods-woman** – try twists, dampers (twist dough cooked in a frying pan), kebabs, chocolate bananas and stuffed apples.

□ **Discover the past** – have an archaeological dig. Find a site that you may dig, such as a patch of garden before planting. Ask permission to dig first! What sort of objects did you find? What do they tell you about the 'site'? (Note: never do any digging anywhere near a proper archaeological site – you can do a lot of damage.)

□ **Have a place-name search.** Find out about local names – street names, pub names, local parks, open spaces and nearby towns. Are they based on local people and events or do they date further back in

the history of the area? Where did your town get its name from?

□ **Have you got a canal near you?** Take a trip on a barge. What was the canal used for in the past? How is it used today? Where does the canal go? Trace its route on a map.

ORIENTEERING

If you can use a map and compass, you can take part in orienteering, which is a race against the clock from check-point to check-point, usually walking or running. In Guide orienteering you work in pairs or teams although if you got really interested and entered

competitions you'd probably have to race on your own. It helps if you are reasonably fit! Lots of camp sites have orienteering courses where you can try your skills.

WIDE GAMES

A wide game is simply a game played in a large space. You can play in built-up areas or more rural surroundings. Here's a wide game played by Guides in Canada. You'll find lots of others in the books *Wide Games* and *Wide Games Two* – buy or borrow copies for your Patrol box!

DEFEAT THE DRAGON

This is a wide game about a school of little dragons and people who would like to get rid of them before they get big and fierce.

Half the players are **Big Dragons** and half are **Dragon Slayers**. You need a number of balloons to be Little Dragons – long green ones are most dragon-like.

The game leaders blow up the balloons and tie a string to each. They place them around the playing area, tying the strings to branches or putting them under rocks. Strings should be tied loosely so that the knot can be untied quickly.

The Big Dragons and Dragon Slayers start as far apart as possible, at opposite ends of the playing area. A small area somewhere between is marked apart as the 'Dragon School'.

The Big Dragons try to find balloons and take them to the Dragon School. The Dragon Slayers try to find and burst the balloons before they are found by Big Dragons. Once a Big Dragon has a balloon in her hand it may not be burst by a Dragon Slayer. (She's afraid of the Big Dragon!)

If a balloon happens to break while being carried to the Dragon School by a Big Dragon, it's counted as a dead dragon.

The game ends when all the little dragons have been found. Who was more successful – the Big Dragons or the Dragon Slayers?

If you play this in a wooded area you can practise camouflage by putting the balloons where they are hard to spot because they blend in with their surroundings.

Make sure no bits of string or balloons are left behind!

(From *Let's Try It*, published by the Girl Guides of Canada)

SAFETY FOR WIDE GAMES:

● Set definite boundaries and make sure everyone knows where they are, and make dangerous, dark or lonely places out-of-bounds
● Play in small groups – never leave anyone on her own
● Use a whistle signal for the end of the game and to tell everyone to come back to base for any reason
● Don't start until everyone understands the game

PIONEERING
Strophanger

THE STROPHANGER

Bridge

Rope ladder

Raft

Make a miniature raft with 35mm film containers and dowelling. Little Ted could be captain!

ENJOYING THE WATER

Water activities are fun! Get going – get afloat! Try ...

☐ **Canoeing** – indoors and outdoors at swimming pools or activity centres

☐ **Rafting** – if you have safe water nearby, build rafts and race!

☐ **Pond dipping** – identify insects, tiny fish, plants. Make a waterscope and look at the wildlife – use a plastic tube with clear plastic film stretched over one end

☐ **Beach walking** – explore the shoreline, rock pools or harbours

☐ **Swimming** – learn how if you can't already. If you can swim, improve your speed or technique or learn life-saving

☐ **Rowing** – single-handed or as a crew. See *The Outdoor Manual* for boat orders

☐ **Take a trip on a riverboat**

☐ **Learn capsize drill**

☐ **Sailing** – on reservoirs, lakes or the sea

☐ **Holiday afloat** on a canal barge

DRY FUN NEAR WATER

☐ **Dry-stone walling** (you'll find suitable stones on a

beach or near a river)

☐ **Organize a sand castle competition** for your Patrol or unit

☐ **Have beach Olympics**

☐ **Practise throwing a rescue line** to reach someone 10 metres away

☐ **Find out about the international flag alphabet** used by shipping. Make badges spelling your names. Each alphabet flag stands for a whole message as well – can you apply any of them to Guiding?

HIKING
Most Guide hikes will be day hikes:
- from camp, round a 'circular' route
- from a railway station or coach drop-off point, either on a circular route or to another point to catch a train, bus or coach back home
- from your home or meeting place outwards and back again

For this sort of hike you will need to
- decide where you are going and plan your route
- wear the right clothes for the activity and the weather
- pack your bag or rucsac with food, map and compass, extra clothes for weather changes and emergencies
- leave a route plan behind you

WHERE ARE WE GOING?
Look at a map of your local area and decide where you would like to go. For a day hike, try not to walk more than six miles to start with – that will give you time to look around you as you travel.

Plan your route! Break it up into stages and choose 'goals' to walk to if you can, like this: 'We'll start at the bus stop … then we'll walk to the harbour … then we'll go over the bridge to the castle and have our sandwiches. After that we'll walk along the coast to Pilgrim's Rocks … then we'll follow the path to the village and catch the bus home.'

What shall I wear?
Summer wear
sunhat and sunscreen
- t-shirt under long sleeved shirt, jumper in pack
- cotton/cotton mix fabrics are better than synthetics as they let perspiration evaporate
- shorts or lightweight trousers

Winter/bad weather wear

- woolly hat and scarf and gloves (waterproof mitts over wool gloves)
- warm jacket or parka over a sweater over long sleeved cotton shirt. Wool is good because it traps lots of air in its fibres. Wear several thin layers, not one thick one
- warm trousers. Don't wear jeans – they get cold, uncomfortable and heavy when wet
- two pairs of woollen socks – long socks protect you from undergrowth and bushes
- strong shoes or boots – trainers will do for short walks but you're much better in proper hiking boots to support your ankles.

For cold and wet weather you need a waterproof kagoule and, if you can get them, overtrousers or gaiters. A brightly coloured kagoule or rucsac is useful for if you ever need to attract attention.

The most important thing to remember is – stay comfortable! Think ahead – put on your kagoule when you can see the rain coming, not when it arrives! Take off your jumper when you are beginning to get hot, put it back on before you get cold.

FEET

When you hike you'll find out just how important your feet are! Always wear comfortable boots or strong shoes for hiking – if you have new boots or shoes break them in by wearing them for short periods before using them for long walks.

Wear socks that fit you and allow your toes to wiggle inside your boots – woollen ones are best. Before you put your socks on, dust your feet with talc, and always carry a spare pair – you can give your feet a new lease of life simply by changing socks! If your boots are big enough wear a pair of thin socks under a thick pair – it's a good way of preventing blisters.

Look after your feet carefully, and if your shoes rub and your foot gets sore, stop and put on a plaster to prevent a blister. You can buy 'moleskin' plasters, which help prevent blisters, from the chemist.

WHAT WILL WE TAKE?

You will need to carry everything you need on your back, so a light comfortable rucsac is best. Borrow or buy a small day sac big enough to carry your lunch, waterproofs, spare socks and woolly, map and compass.

Each Guide should take:

Between your Patrol/group — share it out!

First aid kit

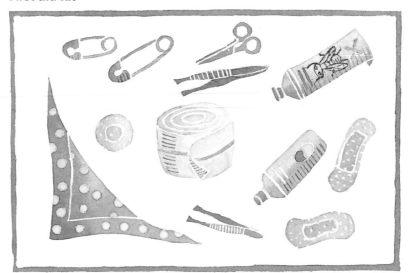

ON THE HIKE

● **Walk at an easy pace,** keeping the group together – no running off ahead, no leaving anyone behind. If anyone has a problem, (e.g. has to tie a bootlace or wants to put a jumper on) everyone should stop and wait until she is ready again.

● **Take short rests** often rather than one long one – and remember it's easier to walk if you've got a rhythm going.

● **If you can, stick to your route plan,** but don't worry if you have to change it for any reason (e.g. weather, blisters, something to see) – it's a guide, not a straitjacket!

● **Take nothing** but photographs, leave nothing but your thanks.

IN AN EMERGENCY

● If the weather has changed, or you end up somewhere you didn't intend to be, or for some other reason you need someone to come out and pick you up, you should stay together and walk to the nearest phone box (or a house with a phone). Ring your Guider or someone's parents, tell them exactly where you are and stay by the phone box until they come to pick you up. Keep warm and dry – dig into your emergency food if you like.

• If someone is hurt or cannot walk any further, get her into shelter and keep her warm. Give first aid if necessary. Leave one person with her while the other two plot a route to the nearest telephone or other help and walk to it.

• For an accident, dial 999 and ask for an ambulance or the Mountain Rescue Service if you are in their area. Give the position and grid reference of where the casualty is and give detail of the injury if you can. Stay by the telephone until the emergency service arrives. Ring your Guider and/or 'home contact' and inform them.

• Keep morale up – sing songs, tell jokes, plan your ideal holiday.

It's important that you keep safe and dry and tell people what you are doing – no-one will mind rescuing you if you've used your common sense!

IDEAS FOR HIKES:

☐ **Incident hike** – an ordinary hike, except you keep coming across things to do on the route – like first aid, choosing camp fire songs, solving puzzles, helping someone who is lost, and other things. This is something which needs setting up in advance – ask your Guider for help!

☐ **Go on an early morning/ dawn hike.**

☐ **Go on a night hike** and sleep in a church hall, Guide hut or someone's home for the rest of the night.

☐ **Hike to a place of interest,** such as the beach, a view point, a ruined castle, or along an ancient way.

☐ **Hike to your local camp site** and have a barbecue.

☐ **Go on a cycle hike** – take your bikes on the train and cycle around your destination, or plan a route home.

Safety note – in some areas you may need to have an adult with you – ask your Guider or parent to join a you.

EXPLORING THE NATURAL WORLD

You might think from all the activities you can do in the out-of-doors that it's a great big adventure playground! Well, that's true up to a point, but you should remember that we share the earth with all kinds of other living things and it's important that we live in harmony with them.

All living things are found in a thin strip above and below the surface of the earth called the **biosphere**. The study of how animals and plants live in this thin strip is called **ecology**. Ecologists look at the way that all living things – including humans – live together in a special balance. When something happens to one animal or plant it may have an effect on many others.

TREES

Investigate a tree to find out just how much different animals and plants depend on each other for life. Look around your neighbourhood – even in the most built-up area you should be able to find a tree.

Native trees have been growing in the British Isles for thousands of years. Many insects and other small animals depend on these trees for food.

SOME COMMON NATIVE TREES

English Oak
Common Beech
Common Ash
Scots Pine
Silver Birch
Crab apple
Hawthorn
Common Hazel
Holly
Rowan
White Willow
Horse Chestnut

OAK

BEECH

SCOTS PINE

SILVER BIRCH

ASH

HOLLY

HAWTHORN

ROWAN

CRAB APPLE

HORSE CHESTNUT

Some trees are not native to the British Isles, but were brought here by travellers and horti-culturalists. These include:
Sycamore
Plane
Fir
Sweet chestnut
Larch
Caucasian
Lime

the great outdoors

GETTING TO KNOW YOUR TREE

Choose a tree and use your senses to get to know it really well.

– Stand back and look at it: silhouette, leaf shape, colours, the way it moves in the breeze

– Hug your tree; can you put your arms around it? Feel the bark with your hands, your cheek and any other part of your body. Is it smooth or rough? Does it have large nooks and crannies, or small dents and holes?

– Has it a distinctive smell? Flowers? Leaves?

– Sit underneath it and listen to the sound of the wind in the leaves

– It's best to leave tasting until you know whether or not it's poisonous!

Introduce a friend to your tree, or share it with someone else. Suggest places for her to touch and smell the tree.

As a Patrol or unit, work in twos and lead your blindfolded partner to any tree. Let her explore it by touch and smell, then lead her away. Can she find the tree again without the blindfold? (You will find she needs to use her sense of touch and smell to find it again.) Set clear borders for this activity.

Use a reference book to find out everything you can about your tree.

LIFE IN AND AROUND YOUR TREE

Find out which animals use your tree for food and shelter by observing them. Identify them using a field guide and list them in groups, such as spiders, worms, slugs, flies etc. Note which part of the tree or its surroundings you have seen them in. See if you can work out what they are feeding on.

Rotting branches and leaves around your tree will be filled with living things. A decomposing log is food for fungi and insects. They help to turn the rotting leaves and branches into soil. Spiders, termites and birds come to feed on the insects. Most of the animals you find on the ground can be gently picked up. When you collect creatures, remember:

● Always handle the animals with great care because it is very easy to damage them.

● When you have finished your investigation, put them back in the place where you found them.

● Finally, don't forget these animals are essential: not only to the other animals which feed on them, but to us as well.

BIRD LIFE

Which birds visit your tree to feed or roost? Write down descriptions of the birds you see and use a field guide to find out what they are. Borrow a pair of binoculars if you can to help see the birds more clearly.

Guess the size of an unknown bird by comparing it with birds you do know. Is it the size of a sparrow, a blackbird, or a crow? Make a note of the bird's colour, particularly any bright colours on its wings or head. The shape of its beak is important as this shows what the bird eats.

SWALLOW

GREAT TIT

BLACKBIRD

Bullfinch – seed eater, large stubby bill.

Robin – insect eater, thinner bill for exploring nooks and crannies.

Hawk/owl – meat eater, hooked bill for ripping prey.

Woodpeckers – a strong, stout bill for breaking up wood to find grubs.

Carrion crow – a general-purpose bill.

Sometimes you can identify a bird by its flight.
Finches have a very bouncy flight, kestrels hover and flycatchers spend much of their time swooping back and forth from a lookout branch, catching insects.

Bird song is also very distinctive. Try imitating bird songs and, if you are not very musical, try putting words to them. Some examples are:

great tit – 'teacher, teacher, teacher'

woodpigeon – 'take two, you, take two'

song thrush – 'did you do it. did you do it. you did, you did.' (Your library might have tapes of bird songs you can borrow.)

Even when there are no birds on your tree you may still find evidence of them. Nests in the branches and holes in the tree trunk are obvious clues. Look underneath your tree as well. Feathers and bird droppings show birds have visited your tree. You may be lucky enough to find an owl's pellet. Owls swallow small mammals and birds whole and then cough up the fur, feathers and bones in a small oval pellet. If you find a pellet, dissect it to find out what the owl has been eating.

Birdwatching is fun to do, but does require patience. The best time of day to observe birds is early morning, late afternoon or early evening when most birds are searching for food. Use your stalking techniques to blend into the background.

HAWK · BULLFINCH · WOODPECKER

THE LIVING TREE

Now you've discovered all about the different parts of your tree, put it all together. Draw a silhouette of your tree. Mark on the outline the correct place of the animals and plants you found in and around your tree. Add to the list below to get a complete picture of life in your tree.

Woodpecker, mouse, spider, blue tit, tawny owl, squirrel, woodlice, lichen, wasp, earthworm, moss, nuthatch, centipede, fox, snail ,beetle, ivy, fungi, mushroom/toadstool, blackbird, caterpillar.

See how your tree is a community for animals, insects and plants. Next to each living organism on your outline make a note (in a different colour) of the type of food it eats.

If the creature eats:

Meat (i.e. other animals) – put C for carnivore

Plants – put H for herbivore

Insects – put I for insectivore

Dead plants and animals – put a D for decomposer

If it is a live green plant – put a P for producer.

PLAY THE FOOD WEB GAME

One person is the tree and the food it produces – leaves, nuts, berries etc. She stands in the middle of the room. Choose some of the Guides to be creatures feeding directly from the tree (such as squirrels, caterpillars, flies, earthworms). Then stand close to the person in the middle. Connect each of them to the tree with string – and you have started your web.

Other Guides now become the predators around the tree. These are animals feeding on other animals. Try to connect all your friends several times with string.

This game can produce some very complicated webs. Can you include human beings in your food web? What would happen to all the animal life if the tree was cut down?

THE PEOPLE EFFECT

The earth depends on individuals being concerned about their environment, thinking carefully about the way they live and acting in a caring and thoughtful way. As someone who cares about the environment you are very important.

Here are some ways you can help to protect your local environment and therefore help the world:

☐ **We can all be more conscious of wasting resources** such as energy, water and materials. Switching off lights, the TV and the radio when they are not needed, making sure doors are shut to keep in heat, are simple, everyday actions that will conserve valuable energy. If you turn off the tap while brushing your teeth you could save up to 25 litres of water a week! Make a poster to hang by a light switch or tap to remind people to conserve energy.

☐ **Think about what you buy,** whether it's sweets, food, clothes or make-up. Some aerosols still contain chemicals which damage the protective layer of ozone around the world. Make-up, creams and lotions are often tested on animals. Lots of things have too

much packaging which is only thrown away. Many products have up to three coverings when one would do. So look before you buy. As a consumer, you have an effect!

☐ **Who does the weekly shop for your household?** Try and influence them to think about the

environment when they go shopping. Recycled toilet roll, environmentally friendly cleaners and detergents, lead free petrol are just some of the things they could change to.

♣ **Does your town have a recycling scheme?** Separate recyclable household waste, such as bottles, newspapers and aluminium cans, and take them along to the recycling unit. Your Guide Company could collect aluminium to sell to raise funds.

☐ **How do you travel?** Do you always get a lift to school or to

Guides? Could you switch to a much less polluting method, such as your own two feet, your bicycle or even roller skates and get fit as well! For long distances use public transport, or share transport, and help to keep one less polluting car off the road.

☐ **Organize your Patrol to survey the area for litter bins.** Are there enough? Start a campaign for more litter bins outside shops, at bus stops, outside takeaways.

the great outdoors

95

♣ Make a nest box or bird feeder. A bird feeder will help birds that don't migrate south for the winter. If you do start feeding birds in the winter, you must keep it up as they will depend on you. If squirrels steal the food, try to figure out a way to put the food beyond their reach, or be prepared to provide a lot more food!

☐ Contact your local WATCH group and find out how you can improve a local area by planting an area to attract wildlife. You may be able to start your own conservation area in your school or back garden.

FEED THE BIRDS!

MAKE A BIRD PUDDING

☐ Write to your local councillors or Member of Parliament about issues you feel are damaging the environment. Is there a road building scheme that will destroy an area of natural beauty? Do you feel more could be done to stop the pollution of our seas?

☐ Join an organisation which campaigns to protect the environment. Some of them have young people's groups you can join for activities or special days out. Find some addresses below – a local group might also advertise in the library.

ADDRESSES

Royal Society for the Protection of Birds
The Lodge, Sandy, Bedfordshire, SG19 2DL
World Wide Fund for Nature
Panda House, Weyside Park, Godalming, Surrey, GU7 1XR
Earth Action (the youth wing of Friends of the Earth)
26–28 Underwood Street, London, N1 7JQ
Royal Society for Nature Conservation
The Green, Witham Park, Lincoln, LN5 7JR

Enjoy the out-of-doors? Why not live there for a while? There's something for everyone to enjoy at camp: new places to explore; living with friends; cooking your own meals; sleeping under the stars; being close to nature; inventing and making things; and lots more. Camp's a chance to do things for yourself!

5

- **You can camp with your Company, with Patrol tents around a central cooking and eating area**
- **You can camp with your Company, with each Patrol having its own space for fire, kitchen, eating area and sleeping tent**
- **You can camp with your Patrol, with your Guider's permission. To do this, someone in the Patrol needs to have the Guide Camp Permit (see page 110) and your camp site needs to be close to adult help in case you need it**

Patrol camping is best — you get to do everything for yourselves!

Imagine your Patrol is going off to camp, along with others in your Company. You will be doing your own cooking and have your own little camp in a corner of the field. What will you need to know about?

- **pitching (putting up) your tent**
- **laying out a kitchen and lighting a fire**
- **what you're going to eat and how to cook it**
- **gadgets**
- **how to cope with bad weather**
- **what equipment you'll need**
- **how to organize yourselves.**
- **how to strike (take down)**

the tent
—
—
(Think of other things and add them.)

TENTS

Whatever size or shape your tent may be, it's your home while you're at camp!

This chapter gives you plenty of information and activities to help you get ready for camp.

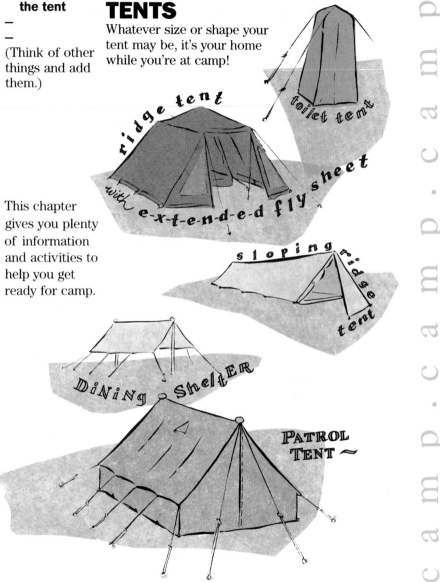

ridge tent with e-x-t-e-n-d-e-d fly sheet

toilet tent

sloping ridge tent

DiNiNg ShEltER

PATROL TENT ~

- Some have sewn-in groundsheets, some don't
- Some have poles inside
- Some have poles outside
- Some have a metal frame
- Some have a flysheet
- Some don't have walls at all (dining shelter)
- Some are made from nylon so they are light to carry
- Some are made from heavy cotton

Most Guide camps use canvas Patrol ridge tents or bell tents without fitted groundsheets. Nowadays many units also use smaller and lighter tents as well.

Practise pitching and striking your tent several times before you go. Use the diagrams to help you.

PITCHING A RIDGE TENT

1 Unpack the tent bag. You should have:
Upright poles – two or three, in sections
A ridge pole to hold the roof up
Tent canvas – unfold it and lie it flat
Pegs:
    large ones for main guys
    medium size for side guys
    small (brailing) pegs for
    around the walls

Dollies – one for each upright pole
Main guys (one for each end of the tent)
At least one mallet and preferably more

2 Choose a level, grassy spot and decide which way you want your tent to face. Lie the ridge pole on the ground where you want the middle of the tent to be. Knock in brailing pegs as markers at each end. Pace out the position of the main guys as shown and knock in four large pegs.

Put the ridge pole on one side.

3 Lie the tent out so that the sod cloth lies along the 'middle line' between the brailers. Make sure the door/s are fastened shut and the front door is facing the way you want it!

Slide the ridge pole into place along the top of the tent. If there are loops inside, use them to guide the pole and keep it in place.

4 Take the upright poles and guide them through the tent so that the spikes at the ends go through the holes in the ridge pole, then through the holes in the canvas. Take off your shoes before crawling on or under the canvas!

Slip the main guys and dollies over the end spikes and untie the guy lines.

5 Make sure the bottoms of the upright poles are still by the brailing pegs. Carefully raise all the uprights at the same time. Each pole should have someone whose job it is to hold it steady once the canvas is up. Brace a foot against the bottom of the pole to keep it in place and hold the pole still until the main guys are in.

6 Slip the main guys over the large pegs and tighten them using the runners until the tent can stand by itself. Do both sides at the same time to even the strain. Check the poles are

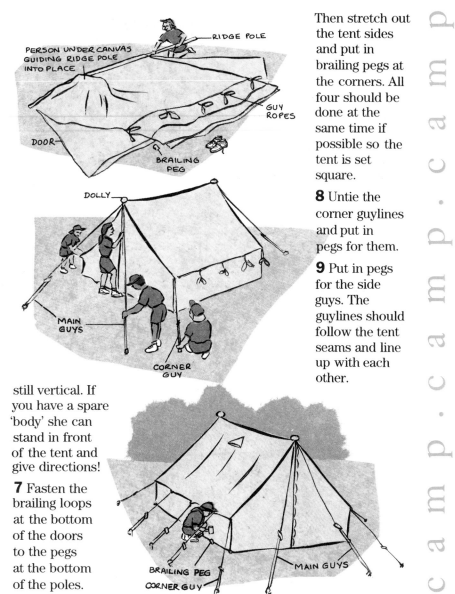

PERSON UNDER CANVAS GUIDING RIDGE POLE INTO PLACE

RIDGE POLE

GUY ROPES

DOOR

BRAILING PEG

DOLLY

MAIN GUYS

CORNER GUY

BRAILING PEG

CORNER GUY

MAIN GUYS

still vertical. If you have a spare 'body' she can stand in front of the tent and give directions!

7 Fasten the brailing loops at the bottom of the doors to the pegs at the bottom of the poles.

Then stretch out the tent sides and put in brailing pegs at the corners. All four should be done at the same time if possible so the tent is set square.

8 Untie the corner guylines and put in pegs for them.

9 Put in pegs for the side guys. The guylines should follow the tent seams and line up with each other.

10 Put in pegs for each of the brailing loops and twist the loops round the pegs.

Guys should rest in peg notches not on the ground! Runners should all face the same way and be about a third of the way up from the pegs.

Roll up the tent bags and tie the bundle to an upright.

Pitching a bell tent:
You should have:
One centre pole
Tent canvas – unfold
Large pegs for guylines
Brailing pegs

1 Assemble pole and lie flat on the ground with the base where you want it to be when the tent is upright. Knock in two marker pegs at the bottom of the pole.

2 From the marker pegs, measure one pole's length to put in four large pegs at A, B, C and D. D will be the peg for the door guylines.

3 Spread out the tent with the point towards B, with the door flaps on top and overlapped. Fasten the lower part of the door and open the ventilators.

4 Undo two guylines on the door and the flap at one side of the door and loop over D. Pull the canvas out evenly, undo two guylines and loop them over A and C. Undo the centre back guyline ready to go over B.

5 Guide the pole into the tent so that the top fits securely inside the grommet. Make sure the base of the pole is by the marker pegs.

6 With two people inside the tent holding the pole, raise the tent until the pole is vertical. Loop the back guyline over B and tighten up all the guys until the tent can stand by itself.

7 Peg down the brailings to form a complete circle – make

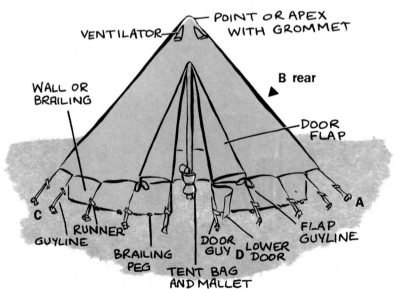

POINT OR APEX WITH GROMMET

VENTILATOR

WALL OR BRAILING

B rear

DOOR FLAP

C

RUNNER

GUYLINE

BRAILING PEG

TENT BAG AND MALLET

DOOR GUY

D LOWER DOOR

FLAP GUYLINE

A

sure the door stays fastened while you do this.

8 Peg out the remaining guylines in an even circle, with the ropes following the tent seam lines.

9 During camp, keep the pole vertical by adjusting guylines and checking the pole is still by the marker pegs.

If the entrance becomes muddy, get two people to hold the pole steady, free the canvas from all pegs and carefully 'walk' the tent round until the doorway is on clean ground. Slip the guys over new pegs and tighten up as before.

STRIKING YOUR TENT

You usually strike a tent by doing in reverse order what you did to put it up. Whatever kind of tent you have, the way you take it down is roughly the same.

1 Empty the tent completely and put your kit to one side out of the way. Lace up the door .

2 Unloop the brailing pegs and take them out. Clean them by scraping them together and stack them in a 'cobhouse'.

3 Untie side guys and tie them up. Take out pegs, clean and stack them. (If you have a ridge tent, someone should be holding the pole steady while this is going on.)

4 (Ridge tent) With someone holding each upright steady, unloosen the main guys and tie them up. Take out the pegs.

5 Lower the tent gently to the ground. Slide the pole/s gently out and straighten the canvas. (Don't kneel or walk on it!) Brush off insects, grass, etc. Fold the sod cloth inside the canvas.

6 When the canvas is flat, decide how you need to fold it up (look at the size of the tent bag). Roll the canvas tightly and pack it into the bag.

7 Meanwhile someone can be dealing with the poles. Pull them apart into sections and tie them up using a pole hitch. They can go into the tent bag or be packed separately. If separate, they should be

pole hitch

PULL TIGHT AND FASTEN WITH A REEF KNOT

labelled so the next user will know which tent they go with.

8 When the pegs are clean and dry, put them into their bag and pack into the tent bag. Don't forget the mallet!

9 Label the bag, including any information the next user might need.

10 'Sweep' your site to make sure it is litter-free and no pegs have been left behind.

Look after your pegs!

- Keep them clean
- Don't knock them in with rope round them
- Loosen by hitting gently back and front – not sideways
- Don't pull out using the rope – use another peg

The tent should be as dry as possible before you pack it away and often the best way to make sure of this is to leave it up until the dew has dried. Sometimes, though, you'll have to strike a tent while it is wet or

damp. When this happens you should hang it out to dry (perhaps in your meeting place or someone's garage) or put it up again as soon as you can when you get home. If a tent is wet when it is put away in the store it will get smelly and mildewy and may rot – and tents are not cheap!

Things to try with your Patrol
☐ Improve your tent-pitching time. Keep a record of your fastest 'pitch'. Challenge other Patrols in your Company.
☐ Make sure everyone knows how to fasten the doors correctly from outside and inside.
☐ When your tent is up it is a good time to mark the ends of each pole with a 'code' to show which pole sections match. Use a different coloured tape for uprights and ridges. If your unit has lots of tents, label poles according to tents.

IN CAMP

Your tent is your home, and like any home it needs looking after all the time. Follow this Tent Code:

- Pitch your tent away from overhanging trees, fireplaces, or dips in the ground.
- Choose a level grassy spot and clear away stones, sticks, etc – it's too late when you've got your bed down!
- Pitch so that the main door is away from the prevailing wind.
- If your tent has a sewn-in groundsheet, open the doors to air the canvas.

TENT ROUTINE
WHEN YOU GET UP

- Air your bedding outside the tent on groundsheets
- Loop the sides up to dry the sod cloth, then roll them towards the inside of the tent

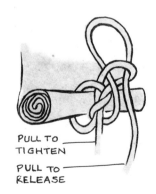

PULL TO
TIGHTEN

PULL TO
RELEASE

and tie them using a donkey hitch.

• Check the pegs and poles. Move any pegs which are out of place, crooked poles can usually be straightened by adjusting guys.

• Tighten guy lines, unless they're rope and it's raining.

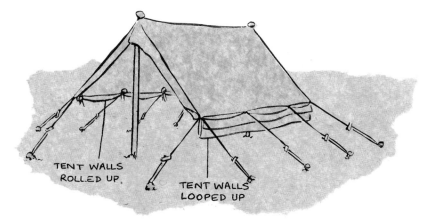

TENT WALLS ROLLED UP.

TENT WALLS LOOPED UP

READY FOR THE DAY

• Keep bags, gadgets and people away from the canvas – rubbing can cause leaks. And never pin anything to the tent!

• Don't hang towels or wet clothes on the guy ropes – it's not good for the tent! Make a washing line.

• Lash a waste-paper bag to an upright and empty it frequently.

AT THE END OF THE DAY

• Fasten the walls back down before you put your beds out.

• If you have rope guys, loosen them slightly.

• Close the back door from the inside, and make someone responsible for closing the front door last thing at night.

BAD WEATHER

A tent can be a surprisingly cosy place in bad weather – just lying in your warm bed listening to the rain on the canvas can lull you to sleep! And your tent will protect you from the elements if you follow these simple rules:

If it rains...

Canvas shrinks in wet weather and, depending on what they're made from, so can guylines. They come in man-made fibre or natural rope, and rope also shrinks in the damp and wet.

In the rain, loosen guylines and fasten your doors securely. Don't come in and out more than you have to – and bring as little water in with you as possible when you do! If something touches the side and you get a leak, run a fingernail down the canvas to let the water run away.

Groundsheets should be tucked inside the tent walls to stop water running under the brailings. If the rain gets really heavy, and you find you're on a waterway, you'll have to dig a trench outside to channel the water away.

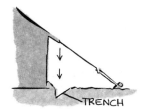

TRENCH

If the ground is too wet, anchor your pegs

If the wind gets up ...
Keep the guylines tight, and if it is raining as well, loosen them 'little and often'.

Secure brailing pegs.

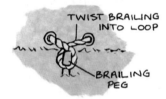

Stop runners slipping.

Storm set.

TENT REPAIRS
HOLES
Patch with canvas roughly the same age, stuck on with waterproof fabric glue.

TEARS
Sew edges together to ease strain, then patch as before.

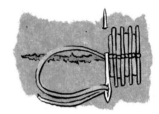

SNAPPED ROPE
Tie the ends at the break with a reef knot. Replace the whole guy when you can.

BROKEN RUNNER
Use a guyline hitch on the rope. You will still be able to tighten or loosen the rope. Challenge someone to make a new runner!

BROKEN/SPLIT POLE

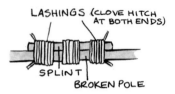

Make a temporary peg.

GADGETS
Make camp life easier with gadgets! They're great for:

• keeping your kit off damp ground
• lifting things off the ground

so you don't have to strain your back
• keeping things where you can find them!

Try some of these – and devise your own!

'raw materials' — broom handles, tomato trays, forked sticks, coat hangers, logs, bamboo canes etc

LASHING TO USE:

Square

Diagonal

Triangular

Shear

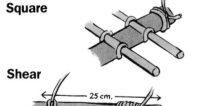

←— 25 cm. —→

TIMBER HITCH TO START SECOND SET OF LASHING

FINISH WITH A CLOVE HITCH

Use string or natural twine – synthetic slips!
☐ Practise making gadgets using twigs, pencils, dowelling, etc and string. Make a model camp kitchen!
☐ Experiment with contruction techniques – which is stronger – a square or a triangle? How can you strengthen your gadgets?

LIFE IN CAMP

There are all sorts of reasons for going to camp – to learn how to live with friends under the sky, to try new activities you don't often do at home, to visit new places, and often to meet new people.

However, to make time for all those things, there will be a rota for all the jobs which need doing: collecting wood, bringing water, cooking, clearing-up, caring for tents, looking after the wash tent and lats (toilets).

If everyone knows what's expected of her and does her bit you will have much more time for exploring, expeditions and games. Some jobs, such as looking after the lats, are not very enjoyable, but need to be done. These jobs are usually shared between the Patrols using a rota, so that no one is doing the same jobs all the time.

At a unit camp, there may be inspections and points are sometimes awarded for tidiness, jobs done well, bedding well aired etc. These may be individual and/or Patrol points and prizes can be awarded at the end of camp.

A typical day in camp might look like this:

7.30	Cooks up and get fire going
8.00	Rest of camp up, air tents, and bedding, get washed
8.30	Breakfast followed by clearing away, camp duties, making up bedding rolls, tidying tents, getting ready for
10.00	Flag break, short notices and prayers for the whole camp around the flagpole Inspection Activity – tracking and trailing
11.30	Elevenses Activity bases for Patrols to do different things
12.30	Patrols or Patrol cooks prepare lunch
1.00	Lunch followed by clearing up and rest hour
2.30	Activity – canoeing or swimming
4.00	Return to camp, and squash and biscuits Activity – making camp mascots, followed by a game of volleyball, then practising stunts for camp fire
5.00	Patrols or Patrol cooks prepare evening meal
6.30	Evening meal followed by clearing up, putting down beds, etc
8.00	Camp fire followed by hot chocolate, wash and brush teeth and
10.00	Bed
10.15	Lights out

Not every day is like that – some days you'll go out for a day or afternoon to visit a nearby town, or swimming pool, or the beach, or for a special activity. Or you might have a survival day, building a shelter and cooking on your own fire - it depends on your camp!

SKILLS YOU'LL NEED AT CAMP
FOLDING AND HOISTING A FLAG

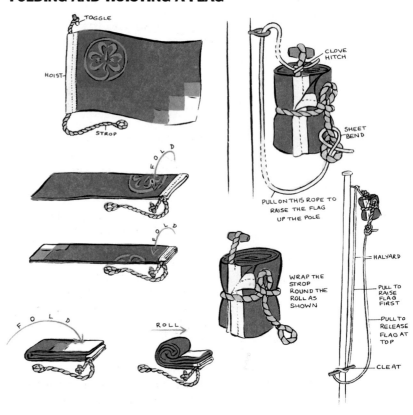

PLANNING REFLECTIONS

When you're at camp, you live much closer to nature and also much closer to your friends. Sometimes camp helps people begin to think much more clearly about their relationships with the world, with their friends – and with God.

Although a lot of your thoughts about God are in your own head, living in the open air and sharing life at camp with your friends can help you to understand your ideas about God a bit more. And camp is an ideal place to share your thoughts with the other people who are there.

Some camps start the day at flagbreak with a reading and prayers; sometimes at the end of camp fire there's a song which is partly a song and partly a prayer. Sometimes you'll plan a Guides' Own, which is an act of worship for the whole camp.

Guides' Owns can be full-length religious services or they can be as simple as a reading, a song and a prayer. (Short ones like this are more often known as Reflections or Meditations). You can include anything which means something to you – it doesn't have to be 'religious'. Before you go to camp, collect poems, prayers, short readings from stories and books that you like. You won't use them all – you probably won't get to plan more than one or two reflection times during a whole camp – but if you have a good collection, you'll be able to pick the best one for that day.

Sharing and *Searching*, published by the GGA, have lots of useful material in them.

WET WEATHER

Shock, horror! The British weather is up to its old tricks again. The most important thing is to **KEEP DRY**. Cover up the woodpile, put on your wet-weather clothes and keep going as if you'd planned the rain.

If your camp has a large tent, all meet up in that and try camp crafts, sing songs, tell stories and get on with camp challenges. If not, go to the local indoor swimming pool, sports centre, cinema or a country house. Don't be afraid to swap your programme about or substitute outdoor activities with indoor ones. Whatever you do, don't stand in the middle of the field getting wet!

CAMP FIRE

Most evenings everyone gathers round the camp fire, to share news and bring everyone together. Sometimes Patrols provide entertainment for the rest of the camp with a sketch, a new song or a play. You could sing part or action songs, tell stories, have a barn dance. The GGA songbooks are full of ideas for camp fire openings and vespers (evening prayers) from all over the world. Finish with taps or even Daylight Taps (page 23).

IDEAS FOR CAMP

Have a theme camp – pick a theme and make everything you do tie in with it. Try an African safari: make African-style gadgets, eat traditional African food, name each Patrol after a different tribe of people, try African crafts such as tie and dye or pottery, have hikes and rambles or treks and safaris, try African songs and games at campfire.

☐ **Other ideas for camps:** pirates, favourite books, Ancient Rome, Wild West, Camelot, Robin Hood … now you think of some!

☐ **Plan your camp to include outdoor activities:** some sites have facilities for things like archery, orienteering, rock climbing, canoeing, sailing, swimming, backwoodsmanship, abseiling – write to your Divison Camp Adviser for places.

☐ **Follow a candle trail at dusk or in the dark.**

☐ **Treasure trails, sports days, midnight feasts!**

☐ **Camouflage a member of your Patrol** and challenge another Patrol to find her.

☐ **Pioneering** – make a camp gateway, a raft, a giant gadget, a swing, a tower.

☐ **Backwoods day** – build a shelter, find and cook your food, make tracks, follow a trail, build a (safe) Guider-trap…

☐ **Make chariots and race.**

☐ **Wide games in the dark** – but make sure no one goes alone and everyone has a safe 'base'.

☐ **Remember those map and compass skills** you learnt before you came to camp? Use them! Plan and go on a hike or try orienteering.

☐ **Make a gift** for a Guider from natural materials.

☐ **Sleep outside your tent** without getting wet (safe sites only).

☐ **Set up a weather station** and try forecasting.

☐ **Spend some time just watching** and listening to the world go by – if you're quiet you might see and hear all sorts of wildlife.

☐ **Try astronomy** – see how many constellations you can identify. And what phase is the moon in?

☐ **Make a flag or mascot** for outside your Patrol tent.

☐ **Make an oven** and bake cakes.

☐ **Lie on your back** and watch the clouds going across the sky.

☐ **Cook porridge** overnight in a haybox.

☐ **Carve yourself a woggle.**

☐ **Make a sundial** or a shower. You'll find lots more ideas in the *Guide Guider's PACs 1, 2 and 3* and the *PIP* cards, and, of course, in *GUIDE PATROL!*

THE GUIDE CAMP PERMIT

With a Guide Camp Permit you can take your Patrol to camp without a Guider, as long as your site is in private grounds and within call of adult assistance. If you enjoy camp, you'll enjoy working for the Permit – it's hard work but you'll have a real sense of achievement when you've done it! You'll find the syllabus for the Guide Camp Permit in the *Guide Badge Book.*

PERSONAL KIT
BEDROLL

Your bed is very important – no sleep makes campers weep!

Note that you have more layers below you than above. Lie on the ground for a while without any layers under you and you'll find out why!

Make your bed like this:

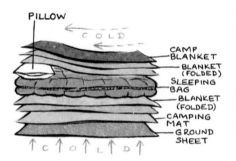

Wear pyjamas or a track suit or an old jumper, pants and socks. If you find you're still chilly, put on a woolly hat – it's the only bit of you outside your bag so it's bound to get cold!

Practical sleeping wear means you won't have to fiddle around getting dressed if it rains and you need to loosen the guys in a hurry – just roll out of bed into your kagoule and go!

Make a bedding roll

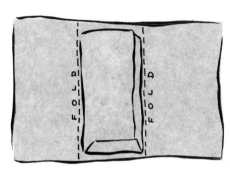

If you tie your bedroll properly
it will stay dry even if it falls
into a river!

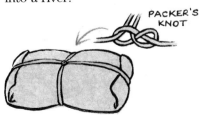

PACKER'S KNOT

CLOTHES AND THINGS

How much you need will, of
course, depend on how long
you are going away for.
Look at the picture and write
a list of things you will need.
Make sure you take all
the clothes you need – and
some spares. Don't forget your
Handbook.

Your Patrol might also want:
An alarm clock
Shoe cleaning kit
Mirror
Sewing/repair kit

Decide what you will need – but remember you will have to (a) carry it and (b) make sure it all fits back into your bag at the end of camp!

Make a sitter

Keep your camera, kagoule, crock bag, etc inside!

Equipment

When you go camping as a unit, you'll need to help your Guiders sort out all the unit equipment before you go.

If you go Patrol camping, you'll need Patrol equipment! This might belong to the unit as a whole so you can borrow it, or you might have your own and add to it by fund raising and scouring car-boot sales and jumbles.

Paint or mark everything with your Patrol colours and find a big enough box for it all. If you can't store it where you meet, try someone's loft, garage or bedroom!

OUTDOOR COOKING

Food tastes twice as delicious outdoors – especially if you have cooked it yourself (must be the taste of burnt fingers!).

Before you go to camp, everyone should let the QM know if there's anything she can't eat for whatever reason – dietary, religious, cultural – so that QM can finalize a menu which will be okay for everyone. If you also let her know the things you like to eat it will make her life even easier!

It's a bit easier if you're cooking as a Patrol, because there are fewer people to accommodate! Plan your menu taking into account everyone's preferences and also how you will be cooking and how long everything will take to cook (you don't want to be hanging around for hours waiting for supper when you're starving hungry). If anyone's religion requires food to be prepared and eaten in a special way make sure the rest of the Patrol knows this.

You won't have a shop round the corner at camp – so plan your menu carefully and make sure your shopping list includes things like matches, washing-up liquid, oil for frying, flour for thickening, etc. Think ahead about how you're going to store everything as well.

If you'd like to find out about healthy eating read pages 41–44. Now's the time to put it into practise!

BREAKFAST

'The most important meal of the day' according to some people. When you're at camp you're using a lot of energy, so it's best to have a cooked breakfast even if the weather is warm. Some favourites are:
- bacon with baked beans or tinned tomatoes
- scrambled egg on toast
- bacon or sausage with tomato and lettuce in a roll
- eggy bread (bread dipped in beaten egg and fried).

You could have instant porridge or cereal, and bread and butter with jam, marmalade or Marmite to follow. Most people usually have tea or coffee with their breakfast as well.

LUNCH OR COLD SUPPERS

If you have a cold lunch you can pack it up and take it with you to save time. Really clever Guides make packed meals adaptable so they can be cooked if the weather turns out miserable.

Sandwich fillings are only limited by your imagination. Try double or even triple (if you've got the mouth for it) deckers and combine lots of fillings. Invent your own salads and carry them around in plastic bags or washed coleslaw containers. Some favourite sandwich and salad ingredients are:
- crisp lettuce, tomato and cucumber
- raw cabbage, carrots and mushrooms
- radishes, onions (the purple ones are sweet)
- cheese and pickle
- hard-boiled eggs and mayonnaise
- coleslaw
- sliced cold meat, pâté and spread
- banana, pear, orange segments, raisins, dates and nuts.

Instead of bread, try using pitta bread; it makes pockets which are easy to carry and eat.

Pizza, tiny pork pies, vegetable pasties and savoury eggs are alternatives to sandwiches – get hold of a book of picnic recipes and experiment!

Labels in illustration:
- FIRE PLACE
- FIRE SHELTER
- AREA FOR CHOPPING WOOD
- STORE TENT
- GREASE TRAP
- WATER
- WOOD PILE
- STORE BOX
- WASH-UP AREA
- AREA FOR FOOD PREPARATION AND SERVING
- SITTERS

Finish off with fruit and a biscuit or cake, and a hot drink – tea, coffee or chocolate. If it's hot, remember to drink lots of liquid to stop dehydration. Water is best but if you can't take yours straight, have squash or fruit juice.

HOT MEALS

You can cook almost anything outdoors that you can cook at home. Your favourite recipes might take longer outside because of the heat loss in open air. You can cook on top of a fire or stove, or you can make yourself a camp oven or a haybox to add variety. Look at the recipes and ideas on page 119–120.

YOUR KITCHEN IN CAMP

Just like in a kitchen at home you need space in your camp kitchen to prepare food, cook it, serve it, clear away and put rubbish.

It helps if there's a 'system' for doing this, so that everyone knows what they are doing and don't get in each other's way.

You will probably use a wood fire or a gas stove for cooking in camp, but there are other ways to cook as well – you can make a camp oven from a cardboard box or a biscuit tin (see page 116), or a haybox (on page 118).

You'll find how to make and light a fire in The Great Outdoors on page 64, and you can find out about stoves on page 117.

FIRES

- Fire can be dangerous
  - Don't wear shorts or anything loose around the fire
  - Use a pot holder to move pans and billies around
  - Don't hang anything over the fire
  - Don't have too many people around the fire — one person per pan (at most) and one 'feeder' to keep the fire going
  - Keep a bucket of water nearby in case you have to put the fire out or someone gets burnt

- Don't let your fire get too big — the burners on your cooker at home are only as big as the bottom of the cooking pot!

COLLECTING AND CHOPPING WOOD

When you are using a wood fire you can learn to know how to collect and chop wood safely.

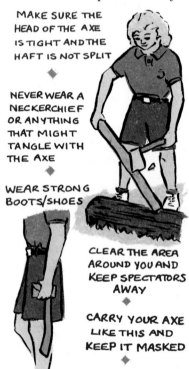

MAKE SURE THE HEAD OF THE AXE IS TIGHT AND THE HAFT IS NOT SPLIT

◆

NEVER WEAR A NECKERCHIEF OR ANYTHING THAT MIGHT TANGLE WITH THE AXE

◆

WEAR STRONG BOOTS/SHOES

CLEAR THE AREA AROUND YOU AND KEEP SPECTATORS AWAY

◆

CARRY YOUR AXE LIKE THIS AND KEEP IT MASKED

◆

Collecting – you will need rope for fetching down dead branches, and dragging big logs. Use a timber hitch.

Chopping – learn how to use and carry an axe safely. Practise chopping off twigs and sawing logs.

OVENS

A camp oven can be very useful. You can buy them but it's much more fun to make your own.

CARDBOARD BOX OVEN

You need:
– two large cardboard boxes, one slightly larger than the other
– heavyweight foil
– coat-hanger wire
– masking tape
– knife and wire cutters
– a metal container to hold the charcoal (an old tin with plenty of holes in, or shaped chicken wire)

GRID RESTING ON SHELF

FOIL LID

BOX COVERED IN FOIL

GRID

BRICK

CHARCOAL IN METAL CONTAINER

– a grid and four bricks
– charcoal, firelighters, matches
– metal tongs
– pot holders
– a baking tin
– Fold the top and bottom flaps of the smaller box inwards and

tape down to make a hollow rectangle. Line with foil, shiny side showing. Fold the foil over to the outside and secure it with masking tape.
– Cut the larger box to make a lid, two or three inches deep. Line the inside with foil, shiny side showing.
– To make a shelf, cut three lengths of wire and push them through the open box, about halfway up the longer side.
– Make a flat fireplace and stand the grid on the bricks. Put about eight charcoal brickettes and a firelighter in the container, place on grid and light the firelighter. Using the tongs, hold the charcoal in the

flames until they catch light.
– When the flames have died down completely, place the foil oven over the charcoal. Put the food on the shelf and cover with the lid. Leave for at least 30 minutes.

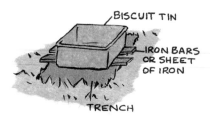

BISCUIT TIN

IRON BARS OR SHEET OF IRON

TRENCH

You will need:
a metal box (a large, square biscuit tin) or a cardboard box, open at one end and completely covered in foil makes a good, small oven
two metal bars e.g. skewers,
a piece of clay or metal drainpipe (plastic will melt), or used tin cans,
a metal sheet (if your metal box has no lid),
a grid
and a suitable place to dig

– Dig a trench. Rest the metal box side down over the trench using the metal bars. Make sure that you obtain permission to dig a trench on the camp site.
– Light a wood fire underneath and pile earth, clay or stones over and around the oven on two sides.
– At the rear make a chimney from tins or a metal or clay drainpipe. Pile the earth around this as well.

– Use the lid of the container or a suitable metal sheet as the oven door. You can use a grid to make a shelf.

Suggested cooking times
Pizza – 30 mins
Lasagne – 45 mins
Cottage pie – 60 mins
Victoria sponge – 30 mins
Apple crumble – 30 mins
Pineapple upside-down pudding – 30 mins

STOVES
There are many different stoves available for camping. Stoves

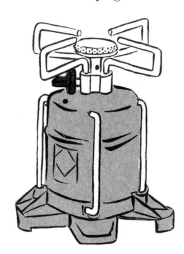

are quite safe if they are used properly. Different types work in different ways, and you

should learn how to use them from someone who knows what they are doing.

There are safety rules which apply to all stoves, though:
– Always use stoves on a flat surface out of the wind.
– Never change a canister or refuel in a confined space.
– Never change a canister or refuel a stove when the stove is hot, or near any other naked flame – you can't see the vapour, but if the tiniest bit meets a flame the whole lot can explode.
– People shouldn't smoke near stoves – even that little glowing light can ignite gas or petrol vapour.
– Never puncture or burn empty gas cans – they can explode – stand them a little away from your camp and dispose of them carefully.

☐ Practise changing a cylinder, using an empty canister, so you know what to do.
☐ Find out how to light and extinguish the stove according to the maker's instructions. Some manufacturers will send you information about how to use their stoves if you write to them.
Ask your local camping store if they have addresses.

KEEPING THINGS HOT

The simplest way of keeping things hot is to put a dish or plate of food over a dixie of hot water and put foil or a lid on top. To keep larger amounts of food hot, make a haybox.

MAKING A HAY BOX

PIECE OF WOOD
PILLOW FILLED WITH HAY
HAY

You will need a solid wooden box, something like a tea chest, or a hole in the ground, newspaper and hay.

– If you are using a hole in the ground, line it first with plastic sheeting to stop the newspaper and hay getting damp.
– Line the bottom and sides of the box with layers of newspaper.
– Thickly pile in hay in the bottom until about half full. Press down firmly.
– Use a dixie with a tight-fitting lid and stand it on top of the hay.
– Pack more hay all round the dixie up to the rim of the box. The hay should make a firm nest so that the dixie can be easily lifted out and put back in.
– Pack the rest of the hay into a pillow case to make a cushion the size of the box. This goes on top of the dixie when in use. A piece of wood or hardboard forms the lid (hold it down with stones).

A haybox uses insulation and is equally good for keeping hot things hot and cold things cold.

CLEARING UP

Clearing up is one of the most important jobs in camp. It helps to keep everyone healthy and it helps protect the environment. If you follow this advice it'll be done in no time!

● Rub washing-up liquid on the outside of pans before using them. This makes them easier to clean.
● Have water heating on the fire during the meal for hot drinks and washing up.
● Fill cooking pots with cold water when you've finished using them.
● Scrape leftovers on plates into a food rubbish bucket.
● Stack washing-up around your table, sort it out and make sure everything is there.

● Wash up in a sensible order, cleanest things first: mugs, cutlery, pudding plates, greasy plates.
● Wash dishes in hot water with detergent using a mop or cloth.
● Use clean tea-towels and put things away in a clean place.
● Wash pans on the table or grass, not in the bowl. Use special billy-rags and not the mop or dishcloth.
● Put everything away in its right place.
● Hang up tea-towels to dry. Use two ropes twisted together if you have no pegs.

- Wipe down all food-preparation areas – counters, tables, stoves etc. Wipe jam jars, ketchup bottles etc after use as these attract flies, ants and wasps.
- Dispose of all rubbish: burn everything burnable (not plastic – it can give off poisonous fumes);
wash tins out, cut off their ends and bash them flat;
burn food rubbish, unless told to bury it;
use a grease trap to dispose of dirty washing-up water;
find out about recycling your rubbish – have separate collection bags for things like paper, glass and aluminium tins and foil and take them to the local recycling point at the end of camp.

RECIPES

Try some of these recipes and experiment with your own.

Shish kebabs

Use a pot holder to protect fingers from metal skewers!

Cheesey potatoes

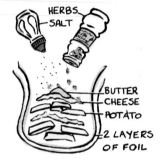

One packet per person. Place in embers for 15–20 minutes, turn occasionally.

ROLL FOIL TOGETHER AT TOP AND AT BOTH ENDS.

Tuna pasta

150g cooked pasta, 2 cans of tuna fish, drained, large can condensed cream of mushroom soup, 125ml milk, 100g grated cheese, 2 tablespoons lemon juice, salt and pepper

Flake the tuna in a can or billy. Add soup, milk, cheese, lemon juice and salt and pepper. Add the drained cooked pasta and mix lightly. Heat thoroughly, stirring carefully.

If you have an oven you can pour the mixture into an oven-proof dish, topped with breadcrumbs and grated cheese or crushed crisps. Bake in a hot oven for 25 minutes.

Beef and apple burgers

500g minced lean beef, 1 egg, beaten, 1 large cooking apple, 1 medium onion, stale bread

Grate the apples, onion and bread coarsely. Mix the minced meat with the grated apples, onion and 2/3 of the breadcrumbs and the beaten

egg. Shape into small cakes and coat with breadcrumbs. Fry for about 7 minutes on each side until cooked through. Serve with onion rings and salad.

DESSERTS

Banana dream boat

6 bananas, a packet of chocolate chips, a packet of miniature marshmallows. You will also need aluminium foil.

Cut an opening the length of the banana, leaving the peel

attached at one end. Scoop out a little of the fruit and eat it. Fill the cavity with the chocolate chips and marshmallows. Put the peel back in place. Wrap in foil, shiny side in. Place in hot embers for 5 to 10 minutes, long enough to melt the chocolate and marshmallows.

Fruit fritters

for the batter: 150g self-raising flour, 1 large egg, 180ml milk.

3 large apples or bananas, or 6 pineapple rings, brown sugar and syrup sauce to serve

Make the batter by beating the egg and milk into the flour until the mixture is smooth. Peel, core (if necessary) and slice the fruit. Dip pieces of fruit into the batter and fry quickly in oil. Turn the fritters to brown them evenly. Drain, sprinkle with brown sugar and serve with syrup sauce.

STORING FOOD

You don't have a fridge at camp,
but there are plenty of ways to
keep food cool, safe and fresh.

Hanging larder in shade
Cool box (cool for a day or so,
but after that good for airtight
store)
Plastic bags/containers for dry
foods e.g. cereal, sugar, flour
Foil wrap/cling film

☐ Make a Patrol store box.

keep milk in bucket with wet tea cloth to cover

cling film

cool box

hanging larder (in the shade of a tree)

Patrol store box
(with water-proof cover)

No two people are exactly the same. From the fine lines on your fingertips to whether you prefer raspberry vanilla ice cream, unique. There will

ripple to you are never ever

be anyone in the rest of the world just like you —

you are absolutely unique!

all about you

6

Everything that has ever happened to you has helped to shape the person you are. Of course, in many ways you may be very similar to other people your age – you may share the same interests, wear the same kinds of clothes, like the same food, but they won't be you.

Use this space to create a profile. Fill in all the details that describe the one and only you! (You might want to use a pencil for some of the details so that you can update them.)

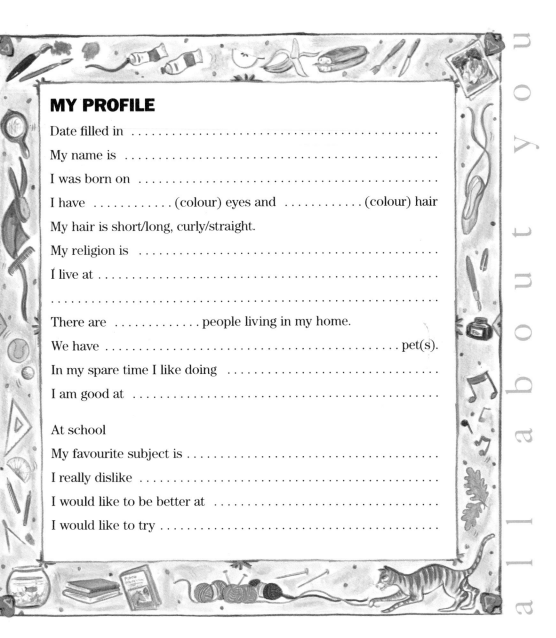

MY PROFILE

Date filled in . . . .

My name is . . . .

I was born on . . . .

I have . . . . (colour) eyes and . . . . (colour) hair

My hair is short/long, curly/straight.

My religion is . . . .

I live at . . . .

. . . .

There are . . . . people living in my home.

We have . . . . pet(s).

In my spare time I like doing . . . .

I am good at . . . .

At school

My favourite subject is . . . .

I really dislike . . . .

I would like to be better at . . . .

I would like to try . . . .

☐ Make a Patrol profile including things from every member, such as:

- photographs
- a set of fingerprints
- tape everyone's voices – individually and together
- origins of surnames.

☐ Find out the length of your stride and hand span. Measure things according to your stride or hand span e.g. how many strides equals the length of your meeting place?

☐ Make a Patrol 'rogues gallery' of silhouette portraits or sketches of one another.

☐ Use each member of the Patrol as a measure. Measure the length of your meeting room/hall.

☐ Guess one another's voices – either blindfold or using a tape recorder.

☐ Start a Patrol log book, with details of Patrol members and use it as a record of the things you do as a Patrol.

Draw a grid and record each other's weight, height, favourite clothes and hobbies. Record how these change over a period of six months or a year.

Challenge other Patrols

Arrange your Patrol in a particular order (without speaking) in birth date/ birthday/height/colour of hair/ age etc. How do you arrange an order for hair colour? Use your imagination!

Make silhouettes, outlines cut from wallpaper and/or footprints. Mix them up without putting names on (number them and keep a 'crib sheet' if you think you mightn't be able to recognize them!) and ask another Patrol to match them up again.

HOBBIES AND INTERESTS

What do you do when you're not doing anything? Do you have a hobby? Practically everyone has something they like to do apart from just being at school or working. Guiding is a hobby – some people would say it's a way of life, too! – but it shouldn't be all you do. List below the things you like to do when you're not doing anything else.

OUT OF DOORS

SPORTS/FITNESS

TECHNICAL/BUILDING THINGS

CRAFTS/BEING CREATIVE

COLLECTING

Some of your ideas might fit under two or even more headings!

Look through the *Guide Badge Book* to see if you can turn any of your hobbies into Interest Badges.

HOBBIES AS CAREERS

If you really like doing something, and you're reasonably good at it, why not think about doing it as a career? Some people are lucky enough to do this – there's no reason why you shouldn't be able to do it too!

☐ Try something new that might turn into a hobby.

☐ Make a musical instrument and play a tune on it.

☐ Go out and try something locally – archery, ice/roller skating, dry slope skiing, canoeing, bowling – something you might have to take a bus ride to.

☐ Go to your local library and find books about different hobbies. Choose one and try it out. (You can also find opportunities to try new things by looking at the notices!)

☐ Invite someone to your Patrol or unit meeting to talk about a hobby none of you have tried (such as bell-ringing, lace-making or playing an unusual instrument). Will they show you how to do it and let you have a go?

☐ Make a model.

☐ Visit an amateur radio station to Celebrate Thinking Day on the Air. Thinking Day on the Air is when Guide units all over the world send messages to each other using radio waves. To find out more, contact the Guiding Activities Division at CHQ.

WHAT'S IT WORTH?

What's important to you? Being happy? Saving the whale? Being rich and famous?

When an idea is important to you, you find out more about it, you can explain it to someone else or argue about it. You feel that it's a good thing, it's worth something, you value it – and it becomes one of your **values**.

Values are important because they help you make decisions about the way you are going to live your life. As you go through your life, you'll find your viewpoint being developed by your family, people you meet, things you hear or read, religious and other experiences, the places you go, the things you see…

Guiding has values – you probably share at least some of them, or you wouldn't have felt able to make the Promise. Some of the values of Guiding are

● friendship
● fun
● helping others
● looking after the world
● being right with God
●
●
●
●
●
●
●

Add others yourself!

FLYING A FLAG FOR GOD

All the great religions of the world have values, too, and the more you find out about them, the more you'll be surprised at how much the people of the world share. Their values are shown in the teachings of the religion, in holy books and writings, and by what the followers actually do. Guides come from all sorts of religions, believe different things and worship in many different ways, but they can all come together in Guiding, because our values are based on what all creatures need – love, help, celebration, friendship, and a sense of something greater than we are.

Many people do believe in God, but they don't share their religious values with others – they feel they can manage just as well without going regularly to a place of worship and joining with other people. It's quite possible to manage this way – after all, you could 'manage' to do Guiding by reading this Handbook and doing some of the things in it – but it wouldn't be half as good as joining with other Guides. You need those other people to keep you going, help you understand things and share the fun – and you need them to get closer to God, too. When you find a place of worship where you like the way things are done, where you hear God speaking to you, where you feel you matter, make it a part of your life.

Your Patrol, your unit, the whole of the world family of Guides and Girl Scouts, all give each other support, love, encouragement and fun. They stick together when things are bad, they help each other through, they share with new members. They sing together, eat together, play together, pray together – not just on meeting nights but at other times too. These are all ideas you'll find in many religions – so you can see how being 'religious' doesn't necessarily make you a better Guide – though it can – but being a Guide can quite definitely help you come to know God and your own religion better.

Guiding works by getting people together who have a lot of ideas in common – people who have made the same Promise, who follow the same code (the Guide Law), who know that the song sounds better when everyone sings in the same key. Different religions are the harmony to the song of Guiding, and Guides work together to make the music God hears sound really good by being better Buddhists, Christians, Hindus, Jews, Muslims, Sikhs … whatever they are.

IDEAS INTO ACTION

It's no good having values if you don't act on them. When you see a harassed mum, with pushchair, stroppy toddler and two bags of shopping pushing along the bus, do you hide in your seat and look out of the window? Or are you there, folding up the pushchair and offering your seat? If your parents get at you for the state of your room, do you huff and puff and blame your sister, or do you try to make sure the situation doesn't arise in the first place? When schoolfriends run down someone when she's not there, do you join in, stand back, or speak out? Values take courage, sometimes.

Things to do in Patrols
☐ Discuss the things that are important to you with other members of the group. What are the similarities and differences in your responses? Compare their comments with those of your family and friends.
☐ Identify the values in the Guide Promise and Law. Discuss them with the others.
☐ Discuss what you most enjoy about Guiding, and why.
☐ Listen to some of your favourite pop songs. What sort

of values do you think they express?

☐ Read a newspaper or magazine article written by a famous person. What sort of values do they represent in their article?

☐ Think about the values of your religion. How do they tie in with what you do in Guiding?

☐ Find out about the values of religions different to your own. What do you share? What is different? Why?

☐ As a Patrol, decide to put your values into action. Raise money for a charity, clear a patch of land, stand up and be counted.

RELATION-SHIPS

Think about all the people you know: your family, your friends at school, your Patrol and your Guiders, the people you met on holiday, your brother's friend who you quite like, your teachers … you have relationships with them all. All relationships are different: you may get on really well with your friend but always seem to do the wrong thing in a particular teacher's lesson. In your family you probably have days when everything goes well, and others where you can't do anything right. In a community – a family, a school, a village, even a Guide Patrol – people have to get along together, so it's worth knowing a little bit about how relationships work.

All relationships involve people sharing, talking and spending time together. When things are going well this is easy to do, but when there are problems you need to make an effort to inject a little give and take.

If a relationship has problems it is often worth working to improve it by spending more time talking or doing things together.

Look at the Guide Law – it has lots of bits in it which will help you get on better with other people. Put a number by each picture to indicate which Law you could keep (or have kept) to make the relationship a little smoother.

family ☐

☐ friends

Patrol + guiders ☐

☐ teachers

'We don't want her
in our Patrol.'

'Go on – have
a smoke –
everyone
else does.'

'Don't drop
litter – it's
pollution.'

Relationships in Guiding are very special – discovering that a stranger's a Guide makes a special bond. You feel you know her a little better, even if you've only just met. And all over the world there are people like you. That's what belonging to WAGGGS means.

In some countries Brownies are called Little Friends. What does this tell you about how they are seen by people in those countries?

Good friends and people who get on well talk together, they keep their lines of communication open and, if they have a problem, they talk about it and sort it out. They can keep safe secrets and let each other down gently, being honest with each other but not brutal. Even if they don't always like doing the same things, they understand each other and make allowances when one loses her temper or doesn't want to talk or come out today. It doesn't matter – a good friend will always be there to listen when she's wanted.

Talking about things is an essential part of any

relationship and, quite often, you can end up having an argument rather than a discussion! There's nothing wrong with that, as long as you don't let it get out of hand.

Try to remember these points when you're discussing something you both feel strongly about:

● Keep to the point – don't drag in the fact that your friend didn't send you a postcard on holiday and she's got a spot on the end of her nose! Don't call her names, either – it's easy to say things but you can never unsay them.

● Don't get excited and don't exaggerate – it's catching and you'll probably end up having a shouting match!

● Listen to what the other person is saying and try to imagine how you would feel in the same situation. When you are angry it is difficult to think clearly. Your body is full of energy. Think of ways to use that energy without hurting other people, such as thumping a pillow or playing tennis. Then think your problem through later.

● If you really can't agree, don't let it get to you. Agree to differ and bury your argument. When it's over – it's finished!

You could practise talking through arguments with your Patrol. Use the situations on page 131 and act them out. This is called **role playing**.

But she's different...

'Go on – talk to her!'

'I can't – I wouldn't know what to say.'

'Look – tomorrow you could have an accident and have to sit in a wheelchair yourself. Would you expect people to forget how to talk to you?'

Well – would you?

Have you ever noticed how strongly many people react to someone who has a disability? They either move swiftly out of the way or talk to the 'normal' person beside her as if she didn't exist, or as if she were a small, stupid child. Not very nice, is it?

Considering the feelings and opinions of others when one or more members of your unit – girls or Guiders – have a disability can produce some very special relationships.

As a Patrol find ways of safely improvising and doing things as if you had a disability such as a visual, hearing or speech impairment or a walking difficulty. For example experience the difficulties people with disabilities have by doing the following:

● tie shoe laces or count money with one hand

● eat or drink without using your hands, or get someone to feed you

● try moving around and doing things in a wheelchair or using crutches.

Ideas like these are called **Cap-Handi** – a Danish idea for making able-bodied people aware of what it feels like to be disabled.

Does anyone in your Patrol know a disabled girl living nearby who might like to be a Guide? She might be too shy to ask or she or her parents might think it would be impossible. Talk to your Guider about how she might be able to become a Guide (by adapting your unit

meetings or by her becoming a Lone attached to your unit).

Think of ways to adapt parts of your unit meeting so that a girl with a disability could take part. What would you need to do for her to go to camp?

Survey your meeting place to see how suitable it would be for someone with mobility problems or who was partially sighted. If it is used by other organizations you could work with them and possibly make recommendations for improvements to the owners.

THE WAY YOU FEEL

The way you feel about things and people changes depending on all sorts of

things – how they behave towards you, how much you know about them, and how you feel yourself. If you can explain your feelings to yourself, you'll be better able to let other people know how you want to be treated, make decisions and resist pressure. Try some of these activities about feelings:

☐ In your Patrol take turns to mime different feelings. Use your face and body rather than words to express each feeling. Try the following: anger, peace, jealousy, tiredness, defensiveness, surprise, fear, frustration.

☐ Write a poem or draw a picture to show some of these feelings.

☐ As a Patrol, talk or write about the best ways to express your feelings in difficult situations without hurting others.

☐ Choose a word from the list below to describe how you would feel in each situation. You may use a word more than once, use more than one word for each situation, or use your own words if you want to.

angry — scared — happy

sad — lonely

jealous — Proud — worried

disappointed

loved — eager

frustrated — embarrassed

suprised — excited

amazed

1 If my best friend moved away I would be

2 When I have an accident I am

3 If I don't get good marks in school I am

4 After being awarded my first badge I was

5 At the start of the school holidays I am

6 If my pet died I would be

7 If I receive an unexpected gift I am

8 The day before an important test at school I feel

9 If I have to go to the doctor or the dentist I feel

A PROBLEM SHARED . . .

Sometimes it helps to talk to someone about a particular problem. It is easier for somebody who is not involved in the situation to look at it more clearly and help you decide what to do. The best way to do this is to talk to someone you can trust – a parent is best, but if you really can't then a friend, a teacher or a Guider may be able to help. Some people write to magazine problem pages for advice if they cannot share their problem with a member of their family or a close friend.

And, of course, if Lonely had been a Guide in her old area, she could join a unit near her new home. There is a transfer form you or your Guider can fill in when people move from one place to another, which lets the new unit know you are coming, so that you'll have a ready-made crowd of friends when you arrive!

Dear Cathy
About a year ago I moved house about 50 miles away from where I used to live. I used to have lots of friends and was really happy. Here, nobody accepts me and, although I've tried very hard, I can't make any friends. They all seem to hang around in groups and get on well. Please help me.

Lonely

Dear Lonely
The worst thing about being lonely is that you start to imagine you're on your own because you're not a likeable person. But, by doing this, you may be making it hard for people to find out about the real you. Why not join a club outside school to meet other people? Try joining other local clubs or the sports centre, where you share a common interest with those involved. The only way to make new friends is to get out and about. Try to do at least two things during the week, and I'm sure you'll get talking to someone you could get on well with.

Cathy

Things to do as a Patrol
☐ Challenge the Patrol to match up the letters and answers from the problem pages of some old magazines.
☐ Make up your own answers to the letters written to a problem page, or make up your own problems for other members of the group to write answers to.

YOU DECIDE
Chocolate or strawberry ice-cream?
Take the bus or walk?
Do homework or go to the fair?

Some decisions are easier to make than others. But ducking out of the decisions you don't want to make can mean that you end up doing something you don't want to do.

B-P gave us an eleventh Guide Law: 'A Guide is not a fool'. A Guide is someone who can make decisions when she needs to, because she gets the practice in Guiding – for example in the Patrol-in-Council, or when she's deciding on which part of a Trefoil to do first.

Deciding whether to swim or play volleyball isn't such a hard decision. For a start, you have a choice, so you have something to do whichever you choose, and your feelings about the two choices are probably fairly clear – you like swimming and hate volleyball, for instance.

When the problem is more complicated and there are feelings involved, the following steps might help:

– Work out what the problem actually is. You might think the problem is that you don't want to go to school. But why? Is it because you have a problem with a teacher, or you haven't done your homework, or you don't like wearing a tie? Keep asking yourself 'Why?' until you come to the real reason. (The problem with the teacher might be because you haven't done your homework!)

– What can you do about it? If the problem is that not getting your homework done means you get into trouble with a teacher, how can you make sure you get your homework done? Why doesn't it get done? Not enough time? – Plan your time more carefully. You're too busy doing other things? Cut down on some of it. You can't do it? – Talk to your parents and the teacher and attack it a bit at a time until you can do it.

Make a list of things you could do to solve the problem.

– Decide what you're going to do, and how you're going to do it, and make sure it gets done! Telling other people what you're going to do will help them support you.

– Afterwards, think about (evaluate) how successful your decision-making was. Do you wish you had acted differently? Do you need to make a new decision now?

YOUR BODY

Since you and your body are together for a long time, you need to learn to take care of it. To appreciate what you've got, find out all you can about your body and how to keep it fit and healthy.

Learn more about your body.

Did you know:
- there are over 600 muscles in the human body;
- that it takes 43 muscles to frown, but only 17 to smile;
- that the largest muscle is the gluteus maximus – your bottom!

Try these activities:

☐ Discover how the muscles of your face work.

☐ Find out how your sense of taste is affected by your sense of smell. Put on a blindfold, pinch your nose and breathe through your mouth for two or three minutes. Ask a friend to put a piece of food in your mouth. Try to guess what it is. Try several different foods, rinsing out your mouth after each try. You could try: apple, banana, cheese, ketchup, mustard, raw carrot and raw onion.

☐ Measure your pulse rate. To take your pulse, press your first two fingers (not your thumb) on your radial artery (close to your thumb on the inside of your wrist). Count how many beats you feel for thirty seconds and multiply by two to get your pulse rate for one minute.

Learn to relax. Sit or lie down in a comfortable position. Close your eyes and relax. Now relax your body, one part at a time. Picture in your mind each part as you relax it. Relax your toes and feet, picture your calves, knees and thighs going limp as you relax your legs. Breathe out and relax your stomach, hips and chest. Let your shoulders, arms and hands go limp, and then your neck, cheeks and head. Breathe evenly. Your whole body should feel relaxed – as if you could melt into the floor. Stay relaxed for a couple of minutes. Count one to ten, slowly waking your body. On the count of ten, open your eyes. How do you feel?

ALL CHANGE

Between the ages of about nine and 16 our bodies go through a lot of changes. This is called puberty and is all part of growing up. Spots, hair, strange odours, it can all be very confusing but it's all quite normal.

Everyone grows at their own pace and among your friends there will be many differences. Sometimes you may feel embarrassed or concerned about how your body is developing. Don't worry, practically everyone feels awkward at some time and this is totally normal – as your whole body changes your thoughts and feelings alter too.

Probably the most important change for you will be the start of your period – or **menstruation** to give it its medical name. The average age for girls to start having periods is about 12, but there aren't any rules about it – you may be older or younger, depending on when your body is ready to change. Starting your periods is a sign that your body is developing naturally to take you through to being an adult. It's a healthy function of the female body and is nothing to be ashamed of.

A period is a monthly flow of blood tissue from your uterus or womb. It can last from two days to a week and eventually settles into a regular pattern, happening about once every 28 days. As each woman is different, the gap between periods can vary from about 21 to 38 days.

On the first day of your period you may feel a dull ache or cramp low down in your abdomen. It doesn't last long and the easiest way to stop it is to exercise (although this may feel like the last thing you want to do). To help the pain go away try this yoga exercise.

The Cat
1 Get down on your hands and knees.
2 Arch your back slowly. Bring your head down. Tighten your stomach muscles.

3 Continue arching. Get your chin as close to your chest as possible. Tighten your buttock muscles. Count to five.

4 Slowly push your back down and push your head and buttocks up. Tighten your buttock muscles.
5 Raise your face to the ceiling. Hold for five seconds. Relax. Repeat once.

Many girls and women have more baths and showers than usual at this time of the month. Bathe, shower or have a strip wash as often as you need to.

There are lots of myths about menstruation – people may tell you not to wash your hair, take baths or touch plants. Ignore them!

Change a towel or tampon as frequently as you need to. For minimum fuss keep an emergency supply of wrapped tampons or sanitary towels in a make-up bag you can keep in your schoolbag or a pocket.

Be prepared when you are on holiday or at camp and keep spare sanitary towels or tampons (whichever you prefer to use) in your bag, just in case. At the same time, you might find you're getting more spots, or your hair suddenly gets so greasy you have to wash it every day, or your moods change violently in the days before a period. All these things are quite normal – and you can do quite a lot to help yourself by eating healthily, keeping your skin and hair clean and keeping fit with some sort of exercise. You may feel as though you're fighting a losing battle, but if you hang on you'll get through it. Remember all your friends are going through this phase too – you're not alone.

ANOTHER WORD ABOUT RELATIONSHIPS

While you're growing up you'll spot that your family – and especially parents – can sometimes have difficulty accepting the situation. You're getting more independent, you've got more of your own views and values and you're changing from the small child they used to have. They might not like some of the things you want to do, and you might feel that they're interfering or being too protective.

At times like this, you've got to remember some of the relationship skills you've learnt. Put yourself in their place – remember that they're responsible for you, even if you feel you can cope with anything, and that they've been looking after you for a long while – it takes time to break the habit! If they disapprove of your friends it could be because they worry about you growing away from them, but it's more likely to be because they can see something in your friends that you can't. Share your feelings with them and give them a chance to explain theirs. Remember they were young once as well!

7

Underarm serve

Overarm serve

express yourself

139

7

Being an artist is something everyone can try. All you have to do is to create something

– a drawing, a piece of music, even a special meal – anything that adds beauty or gives pleasure.

The arts

express our feelings about life and have been used as a way of communicating for centuries.

THE LITERARY ARTS

Okay, so you do this in English at school – but don't think it ends there! The literary arts are things like poetry, novels, and plays. The United Kingdom was the birthplace of some of the world's finest poets, novelists and playwrights. Visit your local library and read the works of others to stimulate your own imagination. Try some of these authors to start with: Joan Aiken, Stephen Bowkett, Betsy Byars, Lois Duncan, Paula Fox, Virginia Hamilton, Ted Hughes, Rudyard Kipling, R.L. Stevenson or Rosemary Sutcliffe. Find some collections of short stories and poems to read as well.

IDEAS FOR INSPIRATION

☐ Find out about writers from different countries.

☐ Write a short story or essay about something that concerns you, e.g. the destruction of our natural environment, your day at school, growing up.

☐ Write a poem about an important event in your life. You could write about the emotion it caused, or the event itself.

☐ Try to write the story of your life in a way that you think will entertain others (this doesn't necessarily mean it has to be funny, just interesting).

☐ Keep a diary or a commonplace book and note down all the things you find that you think are interesting, amusing or express how you feel. These may be quotations from the works of great writers or philosophers, your own brilliant thoughts or experiences, or events and sayings from friends. Illustrate it with photographs, labels or your own works of art. Put absolutely anything you want in it – it'll be an invaluable source of inspiration.

☐ If you have a school magazine: write, draw or take photographs for it or ask to join the editorial team. If you haven't got a school magazine, work towards setting one up or ask your local paper if they want a junior correspondent.

PERFORMING ARTS

Performing arts, as their name suggests, are those performed in front of an audience. Ballet, musical productions and plays are all performing arts.

♣ PUT ON A PLAY

It takes a number of people with different skills, talents and interests to put on a play. Teamwork is the key to a successful play. To put on a play you will need:

● a director: responsible for instructing the actors about their performances
● actors: people who can memorize lines, speak clearly and convey different emotions well
● a producer: organizes the whole play
● a stage manager: co-ordinates the backstage area, scenery and props; gives cues (signals) to actors
● a set designer: decides which stage design, scenery and props are necessary
● a carpenter: builds the sets
● artists: paint or draw the scenery
● a costume designer: decides

what should be worn
- a make-up artist: puts stage make-up on actors
- sound technicians: responsible for sound effects
- a prompter: helps actors who forget their lines
- a publicity director: makes posters and handles all publicity
- stage hands: to change sets and props, operate the curtain etc.

One person can have more than one of these jobs, depending on how many of you are available. All the jobs are important and you should work together as a group and co-operate with each other.

Here are some ideas on how to organize your time:
1 Write a timetable for auditions and rehearsals. How many? How long will each last?
2 Work out a performance date based on an estimate of when the play will be ready.
3 Write down a list of backstage jobs that need to be done and the names of the people in charge of seeing they are done.

Why not make a programme booklet to accompany the play? It should include a cast list and a little bit about the play you are performing. Have a look at theatre programmes for ideas of things you could put in yours.

MUSIC AND DANCE

Music is an excellent way of bringing people together – singing together creates unity and it's an enjoyable way of beginning or ending Company meetings and ceremonies. Select some songs from the wide range of GGA songbooks.

☐ Make up short stories or tales that you can perform by combining acting, dance and music. Try performing myths and fairy tales you know, making up your own music and dance steps.

☐ Have an Old Time Music Hall evening. Learn some Victorian cockney songs which your audience can join in with, get everyone to dress as they might have done then, appoint a master of ceremonies to introduce all the acts, try having a novelty act such as a comic or acrobats.

☐ Form your own Patrol band by making musical instruments from scrap.

☐ Join with other instrumentalists to form a trio, quartet or quintet and perform in public.

FOLK MUSIC AND DANCE

Try these activities to help you explore different cultures through their folk songs and dances.
☐ Learn folk dances from your own and different cultures.
☐ Listen to recordings of folk music from different countries.
☐ Find out if there are any groups of musicians or dancers in your area who are willing to

come and perform folk songs and dances, either local or from around the world, for you.

☐ Discuss what you have learnt about the customs and folklore of different countries from learning their traditional songs and dances.

THE VISUAL ARTS
COLOURS

The use of colours is very important in the visual arts. Colours can convey feelings and moods as well as reflecting the time of day or the season of the year.

Ideas for you to try:

☐ Use different colours and shapes in a painting to express different emotions. Which colours would you use to express the following emotions: peace and serenity; anger and frustration; happiness and joy?

☐ Paint a picture that looks as realistic as you can make it. For example, practise mixing the paints to match different shades of red in a still life of apples, tomatoes, plums and other red fruit.

☐ Which colours do you associate with Spring, Summer, Autumn and Winter? Draw the same subject at different times of the year. First practise

mixing different colours in your palette to represent each season.

☐ Put together a plate of food. Switch off the lights and shine a torch through different pieces of coloured cloth or paper. How does your reaction to the food change as the colours change?

YOUR SPACE

You might have your own room or you might share, but in many ways your living space reflects who you are: your personality and interests. Someone can tell a lot about you from the books on your shelves or the posters on your walls – or the mess on the floor!

Use some of these ideas to personalize your room, bed or corner. Before you start, look carefully at your surroundings and think about the colours you are going to use. Blues and greens, for example, are cool colours and will make your space more peaceful and relaxing; warm reds and oranges will make a cold room feel warmer. Be careful not to introduce too many contrasting colours.

PATCHWORK

It's cheap, it's ecological, it's cheerful – it must be

patchwork! It's a great way to use scraps of fabric of different colours to give your room a whole new lease of life. Collect material leftovers from dressmaking or use pieces from clothes which you've worn out or grown out of.

You need: 48cm × 20cm fabric squares, paper templates 18 × 18cm, a sheet or piece of fabric 160cm × 120cm for the backing, thread, needles, wadding (or some other filling).

What to do

1. Plan your pattern on paper or lay out your squares on a clean flat surface. This quilt has six squares along one side and eight along the other.

2. Sew the squares to paper templates like this:

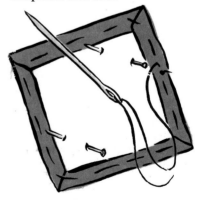

3. Sew the first row of eight squares together in a long strip:

4. Repeat for the other five strips.

5. Join all the strips together to make the top of your quilt.

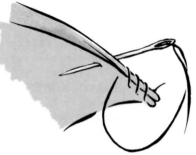

6. Lay the patchwork top right side down on the sheet and lay the wadding over the top of the patchwork. Pin the three layers together. Trim the sheet and wadding to the size of the patchwork and sew them together on three sides using blanket stitch, back stitch or a sewing machine.

7. Turn the quilt right sides out and turn the ends in. Sew by hand or with the machine. Press.

FABRIC FUN

Dramatize your room using throws and drapes. A throw is exactly what it sounds like – a piece of fabric, hemmed or unhemmed, thrown over furniture. Cover an old chair or a table with two or three contrasting cloths. Remnants (the ends of rolls of fabric) are good for this (and are often cheap!) and mixing different patterns and textures looks particularly effective. Try decorating your own fabric (see below for ideas).

STENCILLING

You can stencil just about anything – walls, chairs, doors and fabric. The surface should be smooth and grease-free. Don't forget to ask your parents first – that old table could be a family heirloom!

● Choose a very simple, clean shape: look at different flowers, fruit or trees (try oak sycamore holly or chestnut for example); or you could use geometric shapes (such as triangles and circles), or letters.

● You can buy ready-cut stencils but it's much nicer and cheaper to make your own. Think of all the original and interesting shapes around you –

or go to the library and trace some folk art designs out of books on foreign countries.

● Emulsion paint (not gloss) is ideal for stencilling – use left-overs or buy small tester pots.

● To apply the paint you'll need a proper stencil brush (from decorating or art shops) as a normal paintbrush isn't stiff enough. If you don't have a brush use a sponge and dab on the paint.

How to stencil:

You need: stencil, stencil brush (or sponge), paint, foil tray, kitchen roll and masking tape.

1. Fasten the stencil in place with strips of masking tape.

2. Pour a little paint into a foil tray and fill your stencil brush. Be careful not to overload it. Dab off some of the paint on to kitchen roll – the brush should be almost dry.

3. Apply the paint in dabs, working from the outside edges in. Make sure excess paint doesn't run underneath the stencil.

4. Lift off the stencil carefully. Clean, dry and reposition it, waiting for the first part to dry before starting again.

STORAGE

Decorate the containers in your room (boxes, wastepaper basket) by painting them all one colour. If your room is already decorated in one colour use a contrasting one. Using paint can be very messy, so don't forget to cover an enormous area with lots of newspaper before you start painting.

Or you could cover a special box with a highly individual design by using scraps of your favourite wrapping paper and pictures from magazines. Protect your collage by varnishing it.

IDEAS

☐ Look at your friends' rooms and see what they've done.
☐ Look through magazines for inspiration.
☐ Look at some of the arrangements in a furniture shop.
☐ You might not be able to carry out all your ideas immediately. Start a scrap book and stick in ideas, pictures, fabrics, designs that you like. When you have the time, money and space look through it and bring your ideas to life!
☐ Invite an interior designer to speak to your unit.

MURALS

Murals are paintings on walls, which usually tell a story.

Have a go at painting a mural either on your own or with a group of people. Decide what your design will be before you start painting. Try doing a pencil sketch to scale. If there is a group of you, each person should have their own section, but work out how they are all going to join up before you start painting!

If you can't paint directly on to a wall, make a mural by using a long roll of white paper instead. Then decide the best place to display your mural.

PRINTING

Printing is one of the greatest inventions ever – it opened up knowledge to thousands of people. Apart from being very practical printing is also a highly skilled art form.

Try making a lino cut – a form of relief printing which is the oldest method of printing in the world. You can get everything you need from an art shop.

Making a linocut

You will need: linoleum (13 × 10cm block), carbon paper, tracing paper, white paint and a brush, cutting tool plus V-shaped, small U- and large U-shaped nibs, sharp penknife, glass sheet (or a piece of formica), ink, roller, knife, wooden spoon, paper.

What to do:

1 Preparing: Choose your subject – something simple which doesn't have large areas of solid colour as these are difficult to print. Use the tracing paper to draw round your design in dark ink. Make linocuts from interesting shapes around you, e.g. make designs from local buildings or leaves and flowers. See how many interesting and unusual ideas

for linocuts you can think of.

Paint the surface of your linoleum block white to help the design show up. Flip over the tracing paper, place it on top of the carbon paper and put both over the block. Trace round your design with a hard pencil. Now you're ready to start cutting.

2 Cutting: Warm the linoleum block on a radiator to make it easier to work with. Begin by cutting the basic elements of your design using the V-shaped tool. Clean out the main areas using the large U. Use the smaller gouge and the penknife to create detail. Every cut you make on the lino will show up white in the finished print. At first it is best to cut away less and gradually remove areas as you work. Do not cut too deeply

as shallow areas can be cleaned out afterwards. Make sure any large white areas (where you have removed the lino) are smoothish so they won't hold ink. Cut away the outline to a depth of about half the thickness of the block. Wipe the block clean after cutting.

Always cut away from you and keep your hands behind the cutting edges of the tool.

3 Inking: Prepare only enough ink for your immediate needs. Using an old knife, 'thin' out the ink, on the glass sheet (or formica). If you spread the ink evenly it will transfer evenly to the block. Roll the roller frequently over the inked glass and then the block, varying the direction with each roll.

4 Printing: To print from the block use thin, smooth, soft paper. Place a sheet of paper over the inked block and rub smoothly, but firmly, all over the paper with the wooden spoon, carefully holding the paper in place with your hand. Draw the paper slowly off the block. Experiment with different sorts of paper.

Each linocut makes about 300 prints. Mount them on folded paper to sell as notelets, or make posters on a larger background.

PAPIER MACHE

Papier mâché can be used to make anything from jewellery to masks and stage sets. Best of all, it's kind to the environment because you will be recycling used paper.

You will need: paper – newspaper, paper towels, cardboard cartons; glue – flour and water or wallpaper paste mixed with water (you need about half as much flour or paste as water); and a mixing bowl.

Tear the paper into small pieces and stir into the paste. Leave to stand for two hours until the paper is really soft and mushy. Alternatively you can tear the paper into strips and dip into the paste.

The method you use depends on what you want to make – the mushier mixture moulds like clay and the strips wrap over a frame, such as a blown-up balloon, to make a mask or pot. Make sure your papier mâché is thoroughly dry, then paint or varnish it.

PHOTOGRAPHY

Express your way of looking at things by taking photographs – if a dozen people took a picture of the same thing, all the photos would be different. Pay attention to details – facial expressions, the patterns in a series of buildings, contrasts of light and dark, or cloud formations.

Find out how your camera works.

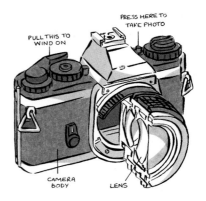

PRESS HERE TO TAKE PHOTO
PULL THIS TO WIND ON
CAMERA BODY
LENS

147

How to take better pictures

1. Plan your photos – look through the viewfinder and see what you are actually taking. Position people carefully against the background and avoid things like a plant growing out of Aunt Mabel's head!

2. Hold the camera steady – keep your elbows close to your body and press the release button gently.

3. Be bold. Cut out irrelevant detail and let your subject fill the frame.

4. To get your subjects (human that is) to look less posed and stiff crack a joke, or ask them to put their arms round each other.

5. If you want to capture the beauty of the landscape avoid taking photos at midday when the sun is highest in the sky and photos look washed-out and flat. Early morning or late afternoon is best when the natural light creates a more dramatic effect.

6. Use an electronic flash when there is not enough light to give a good picture. If you find the flash lights up the subject's eyes, giving them the killer vampire look, try moving closer to the subject and, if you have a flash that can be set to different angles, position it so that light bounces off the ceiling.

IDEAS FOR YOU TO TRY

☐ Try taking a series of photographs with the same shape in them all. Pick a common shape like circles, squares or rectangles and go around photographing everything you can find in which that shape is a feature.

☐ Use a reel of film to tell a story without using words, for example Guide camp, in your locality, a family holiday or a party. The pictures should tell the complete story by themselves. Mount your pictures and display them.

EXPLORING SCIENCE

Science and maths are not just a dry accumulation of facts and principles, they're all about being a detective – asking questions, being nosy and finding out what's going on and why.

OBSERVING

Observing the world around you is very important for a problem solver. Keeping your eyes and ears open should help you solve lots of questions as you'll see the answers in action.

Try each of these activities:

☐ Look closely at your eyes in the mirror. Cover one eye with your hand for ten seconds. Look back in the mirror quickly and observe how your pupils have changed. Why do your eyes react to light in this way?

☐ Make your own rainbow by putting a glass of water on a window sill in direct sunlight. The rainbow will fall on the floor. Identify the colours in your rainbow.

☐ Fill a glass bottle with water and cover it loosely with a cap made out of tin foil. Put the bottle in the freezer and leave it until the water has frozen hard. What happens to the ice and tin foil?

☐ Place a wooden ruler on a table so that part of it sticks over the edge. Twang the ruler gently and listen to the sound. Move the ruler further on to the table and twang it again. How and why has the sound changed?

☐ Choose several objects (fruit, eggs, coins, candles, pieces of wood) and see if they float – either in a bowl of water or in the bath. Why do some objects float and others sink?

☐ Make your own bubbles out of washing-up liquid. Put ten cups of water into a big bowl or jug and then pour in half a cupful of washing-up liquid. Stir it up with a spoon, trying not to make any bubbles. Make four cuts about 2cm long at one end of the straw, then splay it out like flower petals. Dip it into the bubble mixture, shake off the excess mixture and blow very gently to make lots of bubbles. You may have to shake the straw to free the bubbles. Try using different objects to blow bubbles through such as a washing-up liquid bottle.

How does it work?

The washing-up liquid destroys the surface tension of the water, and it allows the surface of the water to be stretched into bubbles, which form when you push air into the washing-up mixture.

Visit one or more of the following:

- a science museum
- a natural history museum
- a planetarium
- an aquarium
- a zoo
- a mining museum
- an archaeological dig
- an alternative technology centre
- botanical gardens
- a transport museum

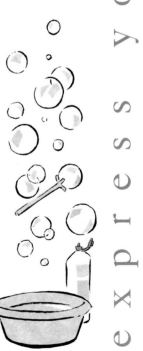

SOLVING PUZZLES

Wanting to know the answer to puzzling questions has started many scientists on their way. By thinking through problems you can make some good guesses about the answers.

Tangrams.

A tangram is an ancient Chinese puzzle. Trace round and cut out the shapes above. Colour each of the shapes a different colour (this helps you to see how it works). Try putting the shapes back together as a square without using the diagram. Try

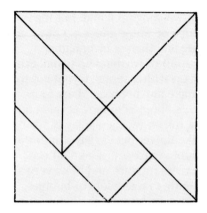

making other designs.

Questions of logic. Can you answer these? (The answers are on page 155.)

1 A big Eskimo and a little Eskimo went fishing together. The little Eskimo was the big Eskimo's son; but the big Eskimo was not the little Eskimo's father. How do you explain that?

2 Two fathers and two sons went to the cinema. None of them were allowed in for less than the full admission price, yet they only paid the price of admission for three. Why did they get away with it?

3 A farmer was standing in a field, together with half a dozen horses, a dozen dogs and six dozen sheep. How many feet were there in the field?

DISCOVERIES

You might be able to look up the answers to science and maths questions in a book but discovering the answers for yourself, by actually doing experiments, is a lot more fun. Scientists often do many experiments before they make an important discovery. Work towards some discoveries of your own by doing the activities below.

☐ Hold your own scientific or mathematical magic show. Think of tricks such as optical illusions which put mathematics, physics, biology or chemistry into action.

☐ Make a toy for a younger child that uses scientific or mathematical knowledge.
☐ Use cookery ingredients to do chemistry experiments in the kitchen.

STICKY ICE

You need: a plate, an ice cube, a piece of string, and some salt.

1 Put an ice cube on a plate.

2 Soak one end of a piece of string in water and then lay it on top of the ice cube.

3 Sprinkle a mound of salt all along the string.

4 Wait ten seconds and then lift the string. The ice cube will come up as well.

The discovery: when it snows salt is spread on icy roads. Water freezes at zero degrees Celsius (0° C) but salt water needs a much lower temperature to freeze. That's why roads are a slushy mess in winter. When you lay the wet string on the ice cube and sprinkle the salt on top, the ice directly underneath the salt (not the string) melts. To be able to do this it has to steal heat from somewhere, and it steals the heat from the water in the string. The water in the string gets colder and freezes, so that the string gets stuck to the ice cube.

SINGING BOTTLES

You need: 2 identical glass bottles, water, a friend.

1 Hold one of the bottles close to your ear and get your friend (who should be about 90cm away) to blow across the top of another bottle so that a note sings out.

2 You should hear exactly the same note coming out of your bottle.

3 Now fill your bottle with a little bit of water and do the same thing – can you still hear a note? Try using different shaped bottles and see what happens.

The discovery: everything in the world – you, your old teddy, your desk at school, a glass bottle – is vibrating. Because the two bottles are identical they vibrate at exactly the same frequency. When your friend blows over the bottle she vibrates the air inside. This vibration is passed through the air in the room to your bottle. (Sound is vibrating air. In places without any air such as the moon, there is no sound.) Because your bottle is identical the same note is produced and what is known as 'resonance' occurs. Resonance is a big vibration which occurs when the natural frequency of the object (in this case the bottle) is the same as an applied frequency (in this case, the vibration of the air). When you add water you change the natural frequency of the bottle, resonance doesn't occur and you don't hear a thing.

When you tune your radio you change its natural frequency until it hits the same frequency as the radio waves. When that happens, and you tune into your favourite station, resonance happens and you hear the music coming out of the radio.

MAKE IT

You can make your own versions of many of the things you use everyday. Try these:

☐ A MICROWAVE OVEN

You can use the infra-red rays from the sun to cook food and prepare a snack for yourself. Microwave ovens cook food in a similar way.

You will need: a small potato, tin foil, a round hanging basket frame (and liner if possible) or a round, metal bowl; a long nail or fork; sticky tape.

1 Line the basket with the foil, shiny side outwards. Make the foil as smooth as possible and tape it in position. (It helps to put a liner under the foil.)

2 Push the nail or fork through the middle of the base of the basket and fix the small potato to it.

3 Set up your 'cooker' facing the sun. To get the best results, you should do this on a VERY hot day around noon.

4 Turn the 'cooker' to face the sun as it moves across the sky.

How it works: The tin foil reflects the sun's rays like a mirror and concentrates them on the potato. The heat warms the potato and should eventually cook it through to the middle if the sun is hot enough.

□ A THERMOS FLASK

Warm things cool down fast if they are left in the cold air because heat travels from the warm objects into the cold air. If you keep your drink in a thermos flask it will stay the same temperature longer.

You will need: a small glass bottle with a screw-on cap, a tin can big enough to hold the bottle, shredded paper (or bits of plastic or foam), sticky tape.

1 Clean the bottle and the can.

2 Sprinkle some of the shredded paper (or plastic or foam) in the bottom of the can.

3 Put the bottle into the centre of the can. Pack the rest of the paper around the bottle all the

way to the top to form an insulation.

4 Secure the insulation with strips of sticky tape inside the can.

5 Fill the bottle.

6 Screw on the bottle cap and snap the can lid into place.

Fill your thermos using a funnel. Compare how well it maintains the temperature of a drink compared with a glass bottle.

♣ GROW YOUR OWN

Plants can be grown from cuttings. A cutting is a small piece of the original plant 'cut off' to grow another one. Ivy, African violets, spider plants and geraniums are all fairly easy to grow from cuttings.

Spider plants and African violets can be grown by separating a piece of the plant and putting it straight into damp compost.

For other plants:

1. Cut off a piece of the plant, just below where the leaves join the stem.

2. Remove most of the leaves from the piece you have chopped off.

3. Place the cutting in water until roots start to grow.

4. When there are lots of roots, plant your cutting in a plant pot with a few stones in the bottom for drainage and fill with potting compost. Push the compost down to keep the plant in place.

5. Keep the soil damp and keep your plant in a sunny place.

□ Make an electronic device to see if your pot plant needs watering.

You will need: 4.7KΩ variable resistor (vertical skeleton type) Transistor type BC171A LED (any colour)
Two pieces of stiff wire 10cm long (you can use straightened paper clips) for the probes
20cm plastic sleeving to cover probes (size 2mm bore) or use sticky tape
20cm electric wire
Two pins
4.5 volt battery
Veroboard 7 tracks × 12 holes

1. Cut the Veroboard to the right size, then draw a grid with the tracks running vertically. Label the tracks A–G across the top.

2. On the plain side of the board, find holes B1 and F1. Put a pin in each of these holes, then turn the board over and solder the pins to the tracks.

3. Cover the probes with casing

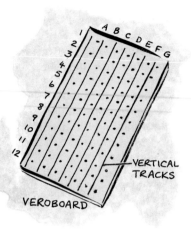

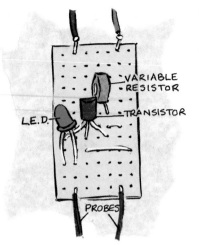

or sticky tape, leaving 1cm bare at both ends of the wire.

4. With pliers, bend one end of each probe to make a right angle. Then solder the probes in holes B12 and G12.

5. The variable resistor goes in holes C5, E4, E6, with the centre leg in C5. Solder the legs to the back of the board, then break the track in hole E5.

6. Now solder a short metal link from E7 to F7. You can use a piece of paper clip.

7. Hold the transistor upright with the flat side facing the variable resistor and put the legs in holes A8, C8 and E8, as shown above. Make sure the flat side is facing the variable resistor. If your transistor has a tag, the leg nearest the tag goes in hole A8.

8. Strip the plastic off the ends of a short piece of wire and solder it in holes C9 and G9.

9. Now examine the LED and find the flat edge on the case (it is hard to see). The leg next to the flat edge is the negative leg. Put the LED in holes A10 and B10, with the negative leg in B10.

10. Solder the LED to the board them trim off the legs at the back.

11. Now solder two 8cm pieces of wire to pins B1 and F1 for the battery. B1 is the negative wire and F1 is the positive wire.

12. Before you connect the battery, make sure all the pieces are in the right holes and there is no solder between the tracks.

Testing it:

Connect the battery (B1 to negative and F1 to positive). The LED should light up. Put the two probes on a piece of damp cloth, the LED should go out. If it stays on, adjust the variable resistor by turning the screw in the centre, until the LED goes out.

How it works:

Water conducts electricity, so when the soil is wet, the current can flow between the two probes. When the current flows this way through the circuit the transistor switches off and the LED goes out. When the soil is dry, the current cannot pass between the probes and the LED stays on.

CARING FOR THE PLANET EARTH

☐ In Patrol groups decide which technological inventions (hairdryer, television, computer for example) you would like to keep and which you could do without. After you have chosen, try and make the list of things you would keep shorter and find good reasons for keeping these things.

☐ Make a dictionary of words related to conservation, recycling and the harmful effects of modern technology on the planet such as biodegradable, recycling, chloroflourocarbons, rainforests, ozone layer and greenhouse effect. Find out as much as you can about the words in your dictionary.

☐ With your Patrol, visit local shops and compare the prices of environmentally friendly products with the other ones. Read the product labels carefully to find out what they contain. Make a poster advertising environmentally friendly products. After you have had a good look at the products and decided what the good points are, organize different people to design, illustrate and write the poster. Your posters should look appealing and imaginative.

♣ Find out what is being done about recycling in your area. Advertise the need for recycling, and help to organize the collection and disposal of reusable materials.

SPORTS

You might not think that sports are particularly creative — but think of ice skating, or a skillful move ending in a goal in a game of netball, and think again. You can play sports for fun, and because you enjoy being part of a team, as well as developing your own personal technique so that you are as good as you can be. Whatever your reasons for playing — sports are fun!

□ Start with something gentle – try playing Jacks!
This is a very old game you can play by yourself or with others.

You need: five small stones or pebbles and a bouncy ball.

Mark the pebbles one to five on both sides, so that whichever way a pebble falls its number can be seen.

Scatter your pebbles on the ground. Then toss the ball, bend down and pick up pebble one with the same hand you tossed the ball with. You must then catch the ball, which may bounce once, with the same hand. Carry on until you have picked up all five pebbles.

If you drop a pebble, pick one up out of order, or miss the ball after it has bounced once, then you will have to start again (or you are out of the game if you are playing with others).

Tennis words:
Many words in tennis have historical origins. Here are a few of them:
'Tennis' comes from the French word 'tenez' meaning 'look out' or 'be ready'. In real tennis, the server shouted this to his opponent as he hit the ball.
'Deuce' means that the score is 40–40 and one player must win two points in a row to win. It comes from the old French word for 'two' on a dice.
In real tennis a servant, tossed up the ball for the server, thus doing him a **'service'**.
'Rally' comes from the French for 'rest' or 'revive'. In real tennis rallies were called rests because this was when the servant rested.

□ Organize a game of five-a-side hockey or football.

Volleyball
To play volleyball you need two teams, ideally with six players in each team. The aim of the game is to hit the ball, using only your hands or arms, over the net and on to the ground. Practise overarm and underarm serves. The receiving side are allowed to touch the ball three times before returning it over the net. Only the serving team can win a point; if the non-serving team win the rally they take service. Once the ball has been grounded, not been returned over the net, or been returned but landed outside the court, the rally is over, and either a point gained or service lost depending on who is serving at the time.

Underarm serve
Overarm serve

(Answers:
Questions of logic
1 The big Eskimo was the little Eskimo's mother.
2 Because there were only three of them: grandfather, father and son.
3 Two – the farmer's. All the rest were paws and hooves.)

express yourself

155

8

o n e   w o r l d

Close your eyes and try to imagine how large the world is and how many people there are living on the earth. Think about all the different nationalities with different cultures there are around the world. Think of people from different countries, about all the millions backgrounds and cultures, all with their own ways of living. You're one of a big family!

8

The more people know about each other, the better they will be at getting on together. To be able to understand people from countries and cultures different from your own, you need to begin by understanding who you are and more about the origins of your own family and friends, and your own community.

Most of the activities in this chapter will help towards the Trefoils.

PEOPLE IN THE UNITED KINGDOM

The United Kingdom is like a huge, multicultural jigsaw – and has been for hundreds of years. Throughout our history our islands have been busy places of comings and goings – just think of the Romans, Saxons, Vikings and Normans of a thousand years and more ago – and, nowadays, our national community is made up of people from all over the world and, especially, the Commonwealth. Everyone who lives in the UK today is a part of the jigsaw pattern, and as Guides – members of one worldwide family – we are some of the people who help make the jigsaw pieces fit together.

Even if you live in an area you feel isn't 'multicultural', just take a look around your house, in the fridge or on your TV screen. Can you really say that everything you do, wear, say or eat comes from just one culture? Even a humble tin of spaghetti comes from another European country. TV, supermarkets, the European Community, music, clothes – all bring the world closer to your home. You are part of the multicultural fabric whether you like it or not.

Here are some activities to try:
☐ Find out about your own history. Where has your family come from? How far back can you take your family tree?
☐ Talk to someone in your community about what life was like fifty years ago. What has changed? Is anything still the same? What were they doing when they were your age? What was the fashion then?
☐ Look at your community through the eyes of someone living in another country. You could put together a scrapbook which describes your community for this person. Try to include such things as: different types of houses, travel, what food is grown locally and local dishes, how people earn a living, what it is like to grow up in your community (schooling, 'clubs' such as Scouting and Guiding, sports and home life), what people enjoy doing, and how your community has changed. You could then use this for international visitors, as a display, or as preparation for going abroad yourself.
☐ In your Patrol, write a play, using puppets or acting out the parts yourself, about some of the important events of your culture, for example naming a baby, a coming-of-age ceremony, a wedding.
☐ With your Patrol, find out the origin of the name of the place or places where you live. How do place-names change over the centuries? Discover the likely origin of the surnames of everyone in the Patrol.

one world

AROUND THE WORLD

The people of the world share lots of things – everyone needs food, clothes, somewhere to live and others to care for them. But even the most basic things – like bread – can vary according to culture and country. Just for fun, unscramble the words below this list to find out where the different types of bread come from.

1. Limpa – a sweet rye bread
2. Nan – a cracker-like bread
3. Dgeg – a bread that may have dates, chestnuts, cinnamon, honey, sesame oil, radishes, the inner bark of the pine tree and leaves of rare plants in it
4. Chambique – a raisin bread
5. Colisa – a small, square three-layered bread with seeds on top
6. Lavash – thin flat bread
7. Chapati – a very thin, flat, round bread made of wheat or corn flour
8. Sourdough – a crisp-crusted white bread

1. Deewsn
2. Rain
3. Rakoe
4. Mebulig
5. Prue
6. Nemiraa
7. Aidin
8. Tuenid ttssae fo miaacre

Choose a country and make a collage using pictures from travel brochures and magazines showing how clothes, houses, food, countryside and so on are different from your own. Find out how children in that country spend their day. Why are there these differences (e.g. weather, religion, poverty)?

Visit a supermarket and find out how many foods come from different countries. Or look in your own store cupboard and see how many different countries you find represented there (e.g. pasta from Italy and canned fruit from Spain). When you know more about WAGGGS regions, the EC and Commonwealth you could challenge someone to see how many things they could find from the European Community – this need not be confined to the store cupboard but could include objects such as cars and toys.

LANGUAGES

If you hear someone speak but can't understand them it's very confusing and you feel at a real disadvantage. Even if you only understand or speak a tiny bit of another language it helps break down barriers between you and someone else.

☐ Learn to speak a few words in another language – if possible a language spoken by some people in your own community. Or choose a language that is used in a place you would like to visit. Try learning:

Hello

Goodbye

My name is …

What is your name?

Yes

No

Please

Thank you

Many cultures communicate without words as well. They use gestures of the hand and head. In Thailand, traditional stories are told through dance. Part of the dancer's costume involves very long fingernails because each small gesture of the hand has great meaning.

We nod our heads for yes and shake our heads for no, but often the same gestures in different countries have very different meanings. In many parts of China, wide staring eyes and sticking your tongue out indicates surprise. Never use the thumbs-up sign in the Eastern Mediterranean – it's a great insult. In parts of India,

One world

you shake your head to say yes and nod to say no!

☐ Find out about, and show your Patrol, several meanings for at least five different hand, head or other body gestures which have different meanings in different countries.
☐ Learn how to say 'Be Prepared' in five different languages.
☐ Learn to write your name in Chinese, Arabic or Cyrillic.
☐ Make your own Thinking Day cards and write greetings in different languages.

FESTIVALS

All round the world, festivals are times when people dress up in their best clothes, eat special food and give presents.

In most countries, the main festivals celebrate special events in people's religions, such as the birth of a prophet. Other celebrations mark the coming of the new year, special days such as birthdays or special national days like Guy Fawkes on November 5.

CHRISTMAS

Every year Christians celebrate Christmas to remember the birth of Jesus Christ. Some countries have their main celebration on December 25, some on January 6. And around the world there are lots of different customs to celebrate this time of year. Many communities tell stories about St Nicholas (alias Santa Claus!)

In the Netherlands, on St Nicholas's Day (December 6) Santa Claus fills children's shoes with presents in return for the hay and carrots they leave for his horse.

Italian children receive presents on January 6, which is traditionally the day the Wise Men brought their gifts to Jesus.

In Sweden, on St Lucia's Day (December 13), the youngest girl in the family or school wears a crown of candles and evergreens and a white dress, and offers special buns to people.

In Mexico, people grow flowers called poinsettias for Christmas because of a story about a little girl who was so poor she had nothing to take to the crib on Christmas Day. She heard a voice telling her to pick some weeds growing nearby and offer them instead. As she got nearer the crib the weeds turned bright red at the top. Poinsettias are also called 'Fireflowers of the Holy Night'.

NEW YEAR

The start of a new year is always a very special time – a time for beginning afresh, turning over new leaves and making New Year's Resolutions. Most people in the UK think of the New Year as beginning on January 1, but the twelve-month year starting in January and ending in December is not the only way to arrange a calendar, so there are plenty of other times when people celebrate a new year.

Chinese New Year is celebrated by Chinese people all over the world. Children receive gifts of money in red envelopes and many decorations are also red because it is the colour of happiness. The celebrations end with the Lantern Festival when a parade of paper lanterns, led by a paper lion or dragon, winds its way through the streets.

Make a paper lion or dragon.

First of all look for some pictures of the Chinese lion and dragon procession to give your Patrol ideas for your design.

You need: cardboard, light fabric, adhesive, chicken wire, acrylic paints, newspaper strips and paste for papier mâché, coloured tissue-paper.

What to do: Make the lion or dragon big enough for your whole Patrol to get inside. First make the head. Use the chicken wire to make the basic shape and then cover it with papier mâché strips. Make the last layer of tissue-paper, soaked in paste. When the head has dried (leave it for a long time) paint it and add eyes, mouth and ears.

To make the body use a long piece of fabric. Add on a tail from card and crêpe paper. Join the head and body together. Get inside and practise your lion or dragon dance.

Many New Year customs probably began as ways of chasing away the evil spirits of the old year and welcoming good fortune.

The festival of Diwali (pronounced Divali), which comes between mid-October and November, is celebrated widely by Indians of the Hindu faith as the 'Festival of Lights' and some regard it as New Year's Day. Children celebrate by acting out the story of Rama and Sita's return to their kingdom after killing the wicked king Ravana. Women draw intricate patterns at their doorways with coloured powders, usually rice and flour, as signs of welcome known as rangoli. In the evening the streets are lit by fireworks and houses are lit by lamps and candles, which is why the festival is called 'Diwali' as it means 'a row of lights'.

Make Diwali lamps.

You will need: clay, a small piece of string for the wick, vegetable oil.
1. Roll the clay into a ball about 5cm across.
2. Hollow it into a bowl shape with a small lip in one side. Leave to dry out.

3. Lie the wick from the lip into the bowl.

4. Add a little vegetable oil to the bowl and let the wick soak.

5. Light the wick at the lip.

To make Rangoli make patterns allowing the powder (chalk, powder paints) to trickle slowly through your fingers on to a piece of paper or other suitable surface.

The Jewish New Year, known as Rosh Hashanah, starts at the beginning of the month of Tishri, whose date varies from year to year but is around the autumnal equinox. Jews have a seven-day week, and their holy day – the sabbath – falls on Saturday.

☐ Find out when the next Rosh Hashanah will be and what celebrations take place then.

Muslims have a lunar calendar – one that follows the phases of the moon. There are 11 days fewer in the lunar calendar than in the solar one. New Year starts, with the new moon at the beginning of Muharram. The years are numbered from the year that the prophet Mohammed, who founded the Muslim religion, fled from Mecca to Medina. This is known as the Hejira (the flight).

During Ramadan, the 9th month of the Islamic calendar, Muslims keep a strict fast from sunrise to sunset each day, to commemorate the time their Holy Book, the Qur'an (Koran) was first revealed.

In some parts of the United Kingdom, families keep the tradition of 'first footing'. The first person across the threshold in the New Year must be a man, tall and dark, carrying a piece of coal and, in some places, a pinch of salt. The coal stands for warmth and the salt for food, so that the family will have both throughout the coming year.

Jewish people celebrate many events in their history. One of these is Hanukkah (the feast of dedication) which commemorates a great victory of religious freedom won at the Jewish Temple of Jerusalem over 2,000 years ago. The festival lasts for eight days and it is a special time for children. During this time potato pancakes called 'latkes' are often served.

♣ Make potato latkes

Ingredients:
several potatoes,
1 onion,
1 tbsp flour,
1/2 tbsp baking powder,
2 eggs,
salt and pepper,
cooking oil for frying.

What to do:
peel the potatoes and soak in cold water. Then grate them and squeeze out any water. You need about two cups of grated potato. Grate the onion and add that. Season with salt and pepper. Mix the flour and baking powder and add to the potato mixture with the beaten eggs. Drop spoonfuls of the mixture on to a hot, well-greased frying pan and spread with the back of a spoon. When one side is brown, flip over. (Potato latkes are delicious served with apple sauce.)

Thanksgiving is America's oldest and best-loved ceremony. A special dinner of turkey and cranberry sauce is served on the third Thursday in November to remember the first Thanksgiving feast held by the Pilgrims and the Indians in 1621 to give thanks for the harvest and other blessings of the year.

In Switzerland on August 1st, they celebrate Swiss national day, with bonfires which are often built as high on the mountain side as possible, and processions of people carrying brightly lit red lanterns.

Japanese girls celebrate Hina Matsuri (the festival of dolls) in March by bringing out their dolls.

□ Try making a Japanese paper doll. Use a piece of wrapping paper or left-over wallpaper.

□ As a Patrol make a calendar and try and mark on it as many different festivals as you can, both from your own families and communities and from around the world. Illustrate it with symbols of each festival.
□ Visit a place of worship other than your own faith. Find out in advance whether you will be expected to behave or dress in a special way.

There are so many customs, foods, stories and ceremonies associated with the ways people worship that there's no space for them all here. Talk to your parents or Guiders about good ways to share things about your faith. Remember that religion is a very personal thing and people can easily be offended, so do treat your own and other people's faiths with consideration.

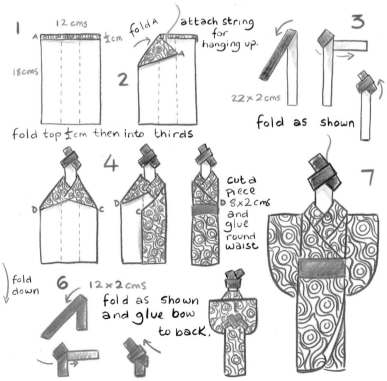

1 12 cms ½cm fold A attach string for hanging up.
18cms
fold top ½cm then into thirds
2
3
22 × 2 cms
fold as shown

4 D C D C
cut a piece 8×2 cms and glue round waist
7

5 14 cms 16 cms fold down
cut to shape and glue to the back as shown

6 12×2cms fold as shown and glue bow to back.

THE WORLD ASSOCIATION OF GIRL GUIDES AND GIRL SCOUTS

Most of the celebrations you have just read about are family celebrations – for close or extended family. As a Guide you have another family, with about eight million members in 118 countries – this is the family of Guiding known as

The World Association of Girl Guides and Girl Scouts (remember three Gs!).

Like all families, members of WAGGGS have lots of things in common which link us.

This map shows where Guiding and Girl Scouting are in the world and the five regions WAGGGS is made up of: Africa, Asia-Pacific, Europe, Western Hemisphere and the Arab Regional Group.

Pax Lodge

Europe

Our Chalet

Arab

Africa

Western Hemisphere

Our Cabaña

Sangam

Asia Pacific

EUROPE

The United Kingdom, of course, belongs to Europe Region. Many European countries have several organizations within their Guide Association. For instance in Belgium they have Flemish-speaking, French-speaking, Roman Catholic and 'open' organizations. On the other hand, in the United Kingdom we have one Association for everyone, whatever nationality, religion or language group they belong to.

Can you name all the countries on the map?

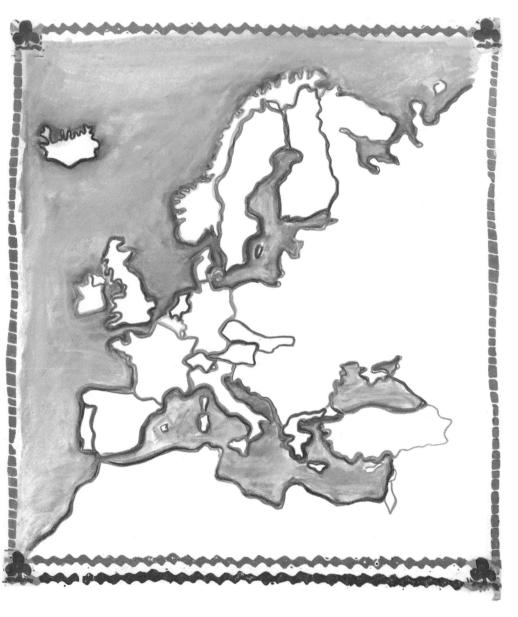

Try some of these activities from different parts of Europe:

SCANDINAVIA

The Scandinavian countries are Norway, Sweden, Denmark, Iceland and Finland. Straw ornaments are an important part of Christmas in Scandinavia. They are always tied with red string.

To make a straw star you will need: thin drinking straws (white or yellow), red string or crochet wool, scissors and ruler.

Cut the straws into 10cm lengths. For each star you will need five pieces. Then:

FRANCE

Marbles is one of the oldest games in the world. This form, called the Serpent, is a favourite with French children. Any number can play, but the more there are, the more complicated the game is!

You will need: one playing marble for each player and a pointed stick for drawing the serpent.

1. Draw the outline of the serpent on smooth level ground. Mark two Xs as shown on the diagram, and dig a small hole for the serpent's eye.

The first player shoots her marble along the serpent's body following the direction of the arrows in the diagram. The other players take turns until everyone has had a go, and the first player goes again.

Any marbles which go outside the 'serpent' or stop on an X or are hit by another marble have to go back to the tail and start again. The first player to get right round the snake and roll into the eye is the winner.

SPAIN

♣There are heaps of things which are good to eat and easy to cook from España. Try tortilla, a potato omelette cooked on both sides.

To serve 2–4 you will need:

4 large eggs, beaten
4 tablespoons olive oil
2 onions (about 175g), finely chopped
3 potatoes (about 350g), cut into 1cm dice
salt and freshly ground black pepper
olives, onion and pepper rings, to garnish (optional)

1. Heat three tablespoons of the oil in a heavy-based frying pan, add onions and potatoes, cover the pan and cook over medium heat for about 15 minutes, stirring occasionally, until soft and golden. Turn off the heat.
2. Remove with a slotted spoon, and put to one side to cool for about five minutes. Wipe the pan thoroughly with kitchen paper or a clean cloth.
3. Add the cooled vegetables, salt and pepper to the beaten eggs and stir well.
4. Heat the rest of the oil in the pan, add the egg and vegetable mixture and cook, uncovered, over a medium heat for 12–15 minutes until the base is set but the centre of the omelette is still slightly creamy.
5. Loosen the edge of the omelette with a spatula and remove the pan from the heat. Turn the omelette over by holding a large plate firmly over the pan (use oven gloves for this!), then, carefully, turning the pan over so the plate (with the omelette on it) is underneath. Then slide the tortilla back into the pan to cook on the other side for 4–5 minutes.
6. While the omelette is cooking, warm a serving plate to that it loses no heat when you take it from the pan to the plate. Serve garnished and cut into wedges.

♣Find out how to cook fabada, pisto, paella or other famous regional dishes from Spain. Or perhaps different types of pasta: ravioli, spaghetti, tortellini or pizza from Italy, or a moussaka from Greece.

MORE ABOUT WAGGGS

WAGGGS has its offices in London, at the World Bureau, next door to Pax Lodge. Here the day-to-day work of WAGGGS, training, support, finance, linking of countries, sharing of ideas and so on is carried out by the Director and her staff, using the three official languages of WAGGGS – English, French and Spanish.

Every three years, delegates from each member country of WAGGGS meet at a World Conference, to evaluate the last three years and plan for the future; to welcome countries into membership of WAGGGS, first of all as Associate Members, and then as Full Members; and to elect one-third of the World Committee. This committee has a membership of 12 women. Whatever their nationality, they work as volunteers to help Guiding and Girl Scouting throughout the world.

The World Bureau produces a number of useful publications including **Trefoil Around the World**, which tells you about all the Guide Associations in the member countries of WAGGGS you can buy them from Guide shops and the Trading Service.

BRANCH ASSOCIATIONS

Branch Associations are Guide Associations which are represented by another country's Association in WAGGGS.

Independent Commonwealth countries are, of course, members of WAGGGS in their own right. However in some Dependent Territories (i.e. countries still governed by Britain) and in some very small self-governing states, the United Kingdom GGA continues to represent them in WAGGGS. Australia and New Zealand also have Branch Associations of their own.

☐ As a Patrol find out about the World Centres: Our Chalet, Our Cabaña, Sangam and Pax Lodge.

☐ 'Adopt' a Patrol in another country. Correspond with them, find out about Guiding, school and life in general. Send cassette tapes, photographs, postcards and letters. See page 178 for information about Guiding pen-friends.

☐ Play international Happy Families by making up cards with the badge, flag, uniform and motto of one country for each 'family'.

THE WESTERN HEMISPHERE

Spanish is an important language in the Western Hemisphere, which stretches from Canada and the USA in the north through Central America and the Caribbean, to the countries of South America. Here are some ideas for you to try from this region.

UNITED STATES OF AMERICA

♣ **Cookies** (biscuits) play an important part in American cooking – and every year the Girl Scouts raise funds by selling home-made cookies. The name comes from the Dutch word koekjes. So why not try and make these Peanut Butter cookies.

To make about 50 cookies you will need:

100g butter
75g soft dark brown sugar
75g granulated sugar
1 egg
½ teaspoon vanilla essence
225g peanut butter
150g plain flour
½ teaspoon bicarbonate of soda
½ teaspoon salt

Cream the butter and all the sugar together until soft and fluffy. Lightly mix the egg and vanilla essence (vanilla essence works better than vanilla flavouring) and, gradually, beat into the butter and sugar, then stir in the peanut butter and mix well. Sift together the flour, bicarbonate of soda and salt into a bowl and stir into the mixture. If you have time, chill the mixture in the fridge for 30 minutes.

Flour your hands lightly and roll spoonfuls of the dough into small balls. Place on a greased baking tray and press flat with a fork. Bake in a pre-heated oven at Gas Mark 4/350° F/180° C for 15 minutes. Lift your cookies from the baking sheet with a knife or a spatula and cool on a wire tray.

You might prefer another American favourite –
Brownies
To make 16 squares you will need:

100g butter
25–40g cocoa powder
2 eggs
225g caster sugar
1 teaspoon vanilla essence
50g self-raising flour
50–100g chopped walnuts
50g raisins (optional)

Preheat the oven to Gas Mark 4/350° F/180° C. Grease a 20cm square, shallow cake tin and line the bottom with greased greaseproof paper.

Melt the butter in a small saucepan over a low heat, stir in the cocoa until blended and put to one side. Beat the eggs and caster sugar together well, and add the cocoa mixture and the vanilla essence. Sift the flour, add to the mixture and mix thoroughly. Stir in the nuts and raisins and turn into the tin.

Bake in the centre of the oven for 30–35 minutes. Allow to cool for ten minutes in the tin, then cut into 5cm squares, remove from the tin and stand on a rack to finish cooling.

CARNIVAL!

All over the Western Hemisphere, carnival – Mardi Gras – is celebrated just before Lent begins. There are famous carnivals in New Orleans, Brazil, and on many of the Caribbean islands, but most famous of all, perhaps, is carnival time on Trinidad and Tobago. This is where calypso music began and is the home of the steel band. 'Play mas' is how Trinidadians describe having fun at carnival – 'Mas' is short for masquerader- a person who dresses up. For carnival, everyone dresses up.

Here is how to make a **carnival mask**.

You will need: 2 sheets of card (different colours), pencil, stapler, scissors, coloured foil, pva glue, ruler, sticky tape, and string.

1. Draw the basic shape, about 20cm longer than your head, on coloured card. Mark where the eyes, nose and mouth will come, and draw shaping lines around the edge as shown.
2. Cut out the mask, and the nose, mouth and eye holes. Cut along the shaping lines.
3. On the other piece of card, draw eye and mouth shapes, about twice as long as the spaces on your mask. Draw in zigzag patterns for eyelashes and teeth and cut them out

carefully. Cut along the zigzags until you have two parts for each eye and the mouth. Then join them again with sticky tape at each end, so you can open and close the eye/mouth by pushing the ends in.

4. Make a nose with an offcut of card about 3cm longer and slightly wider than the nose space on the mask. Fold it in half and draw the shape you want on one side, then cut it out.

5. Give your mask some shape by stapling together the lines you cut earlier around the edge.

6. Attach the eyes, nose and mouth using sticky tape and working from the back. Make a fringe from foil and staple it around the edge of the mask.

7. Staple two pieces of string to the edges of the mask to tie it on – and you're ready for Mardi Gras!

MEXICO

In South and Central America Christmas is associated with the piñata. A clay jar, made in the shape of a bird or animal and filled with sweets, is hung from a string, so that it can be raised and lowered, and the children, blindfold, try to break it with a stick. The game is played after evening prayers. In some South American countries, three piñatas are strung up, one filled with rice, one with old shoes and one with nice things to eat. Not until the contents come tumbling out do the players discover which one they have attacked!

You will find out how to make a piñata on card 1 of Patrol Ideas Pack 1 – you should have a pack in your Patrol box!

PERU

♣ Guides in Peru usually cook over charcoal or in a **pachamanca** (a bean hole) and one of their favourite dishes is **causa**.
To make enough **causa** for eight people you will need:

Potato mixture:
6 medium potatoes, cooked
juice of 5 lemons
½ cup of salad oil
1 raw egg
1 teaspoon salt
½ teaspoon pepper
paprika to taste

Filling:
about 360g tinned tuna, drained
1 cup of mayonnaise
1 cup of cooked sweetcorn
2 avocados, chopped

Optional:
Cheese cubes
2 hard-boiled eggs
black olives

1. Mash the potatoes and mix with the other potato mixture ingredients.

2. Grease a shallow bowl or baking dish and line firmly with the mixture.

3. Mix together all the filling ingredients and pile on to the potato. Level with the back of a fork.

4. Cover the filling with the rest of the potato and seal the edges by pressing with a fork.

5. Turn out the **causa** on a large plate and decorate with cheese, slices of hard-boiled egg and olives.

ASIA–PACIFIC

The Asia-Pacific region of WAGGGS covers a huge area, with many different cultures. Here are some activities which you could try.

INDIA

Puja is an Indian welcome performed in many homes throughout India and at Sangam, one of the World Centres. You could welcome visitors to a special international event like a Thinking Day meeting in this way.

You need: kum-kum (red powder), turmeric (yellow powder), rice, a betel nut (or any nut), a lamp (a nightlight will do), coconut, sugar and a garland of flowers for each person.

The group bearing the offering greets each guest in turn, bowing with their hands together as if praying. The guest does the same in return.

1. Place a dab of the kum-kum and another of the turmeric in the centre of the guest's forehead with a fingertip. This stands for good fortune.

2. Sprinkle a few grains of the rice over the visitor's head to wish her prosperity.

3. Circle the nut three times round the guest's head to show purity and fragrance and help digestion.

4. Circle the lamp three times round her head, to show the light to guide her in the correct path.

5. Offer the guest first the coconut and then the sugar. She should receive the food in her right hand because it is considered bad manners and unclean to eat with the left. Coconut and sugar stand for fertility.

6. Finally place a garland of flowers around the guest's neck as a symbol of friendship.

Then move on to the the next guest!

People in the Asia-Pacific countries use garlands of fresh flowers for special occasions like weddings, as well as for greeting visitors. Paper flowers are not as beautiful as real flowers but they do last longer! To make a garland of roses you will need:

1. crêpe or tissue paper

2. needle, thread

Think of other ways to make flowers!

THE PHILIPPINES

Try this Tinikling or bamboo poles dance from the Philippines with your Patrol. The steps of the dance show how the tickling bird hops in and out of the thick undergrowth without getting its feet caught.

You will need: two poles about 3m long (bamboo or dowelling) and two wooden crossbars, about 5cm × 75cm.

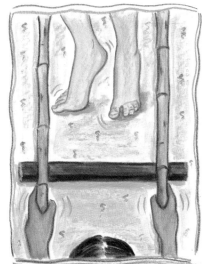

Tap long poles together twice, then slide along cross poles and tap on cross poles. Rhythm should go tap, tap, slide, tap, tap, slide'. Don't lift the poles along the cross poles – slide them.

Make up your own dance steps in and out of the poles (watch your ankles!). It's probably best to have just one person dancing at first, but, when you are good at it, you can try two or even three people hopping in and out of the poles. Remember you're supposed to be birds hopping through the undergrowth so keep the movements quick and bird-like.

AUSTRALIA

Most Australians love the out-of-doors and frequently eat outside cooking on a barbecue. Try making these **Lamingtons** for pudding:
Melt chocolate squares or dots (real chocolate is best) on a baking tray in an oven pre-heated to Gas Mark 1/275° F/140° C.

Dip small squares of sponge cake so they become coated with chocolate. Sprinkle over some dessicated coconut and leave to cool on a wire rack.

On special days the favourite sweet is a

Pavlova

You will need:
3 eggs
150gm castor sugar
1 level tspn cornflour
1 tspn vinegar
1 tspn cooking oil
½ tspn vanilla essence

Small carton double or whipping cream
Soft fruit to decorate (e.g. strawberries, raspberries, passion fruit, guava, bananas, etc)
1 sheet of greaseproof paper to cover a baking tray

1. Preheat the oven at its lowest setting. Place a medium-sized plate face down on the greaseproof paper and draw round it, then lie the paper (marked side underneath) on the baking sheet. Rub a little oil on to it and put to one side.

2. Break the eggs carefully and separate the white from the yolk. Keep

~Pavlova~

the yolks for another recipe. Beat the whites until they stand up in peaks. (If you have a food mixer this is much quicker!)

3. Keep beating while adding the sugar a bit at a time. When you have added all the sugar and the mixture is stiff, stir in the cornflour, vinegar and vanilla.

4. Pour the mixture gently on to the paper, filling the marked circle and making a wall around the edge rather like a paddling pool.

5. Bake for 1¼–1½ hours until the outside is a crisp, golden colour (the inside will still be soft). Leave to cool.

6. Beat the cream until thick and pile into the pavlova. Slice your fruit and arrange it on top of the cream.

You could fill the pavlova with anything you like – why not try a healthy eating pavlova with more fruit and yogurt instead of cream?

INDONESIA

In Indonesia shadow puppets are used a lot, especially to tell their traditional stories. The puppets are elaborately cut out, and sticks move their hands and arms. The most famous story is that of the prince who kills the villain who is trying to take away his beautiful princess, but there are many more. Why not try a shadow puppet show?

THE GIRL GUIDE FRIENDSHIP FUND

As the largest youth movement for women in the world, the World Association is in a unique position. Guides and Girl Scouts are able to visit each other, and often to help each other in service projects, and are able to learn first-hand about the problems which people face in their own countries.

One way of helping is to raise money to help Guides abroad.

☐ As a Patrol collect or raise money for one of the Girl Guide Friendship Fund Projects. The GGFF has an appeal in summer and around Christmas every year to raise money for two or three projects to help Guides in different parts of the world. In addition it runs a Disaster Fund all the year round. Money from this Fund is sent to help Guides in countries where a disaster such as an earthquake or hurricane has happened. Details of the Appeals appear in *GUIDE PATROL* or you can write for details to Commonwealth Headquarters.

☐ Find out what Primary Health Care is. Which diseases most commonly kill children? Why don't they kill many children in the UK? Why is good water so important? Do you know where yours comes from, and how it is treated before it reaches you – try and find out.

☐ Make a list of some of the most common things you eat, or use in cooking like potatoes, salt, baked beans, bananas, corn flakes. Find out which countries they come from. Are there Guides or Girl Scouts in those countries.

As a result of people moving from rural areas into urban areas looking for work and what they think will be a better life, shanty towns (collections of makeshift homes) have appeared beside many of the great cities of the world. The homes are made of cardboard, scraps of wood, old blankets, anything people can find.

☐ As a Patrol build a house typical of a shanty town.

You will need: wooden poles, rope, cardboard, old doors, corrugated iron, stones, old blankets and anything else you can think of!

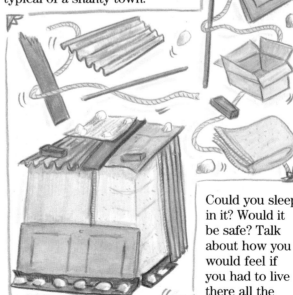

Could you sleep in it? Would it be safe? Talk about how you would feel if you had to live there all the time.

AFRICA

One area of the world which this chapter has not mentioned so far is Africa. As you already know, it was in Africa, at Mafeking, that the idea of Scouting occurred to Baden-Powell, and it is in Africa, in Kenya, that both the World Chief Guide and World Chief Scout are buried.

BOTSWANA

In Botswana, the children make clay cows with thick bodies, very short legs and long pointed horns. They make other animals too, but never make clay dolls.

KENYA

Here is a recipe for a banana drink. To make six servings you will need:

4 bananas
1½ litres natural yoghurt
1½ litres orange juice
8 tablespoons honey

Slice the bananas and liquidise them or mash with a fork. Mix the mashed bananas and the rest of the ingredients in a large bowl. Pour into four tall glasses and serve with ice.

NIGERIA

● **Tie-dying** is an old art that was first perfected by the people of Nigeria. They use natural colours from roots and plants to dye the material.
To tie-dye a T-shirt, a scarf or a length of cloth, you need: dye, salt, a sachet of cold fix, string or rubber bands, a bucket or basin (not aluminium), a stick, scissors, rubber gloves and an apron. Follow the instructions on the packet of dye carefully for best results.

Tie-dying works best when you tie the fabric really tightly so that the dye cannot reach under the string. You can use rubber bands if you want.

Rinse the fabric in several changes of water. Leave in hot, soapy water for five minutes and then rinse again until no more dye comes out of the cloth. You can use more than one colour – begin with the lightest colour and go through each step of instructions for every colour.

LESOTHO

Dithwai is a game played by the children of Lesotho. Each player builds a cattle kraal (a circle) in the earth about 20cm across and 3cm high to house ten head of cattle (ten stones).

Each player in turn looks carefully at her stones and says to the others:
'Let me examine my cattle'.
They answer:
'Have you looked at them?'

She covers her eyes and they each take a stone and put it in their kraals. She then opens her eyes and tries to recognize her 'cattle'. If she is right she takes them back. The winner is the person with the largest herd.

THE ARAB REGIONAL GROUP

The Arab Regional Group does not follow geographical boundaries, but almost all the members are Arabs and for the most part they are Muslim.

☐ Al Henna is a type of make-up made from the leaves of the henna tree, which leaves a dark brown pattern when painted on the skin. There are various designs:
ghamssa- dyeing the whole hand up to the wrist;
al kassa – decorating the fingers
jooty – striping the feet with shoe-like shapes.

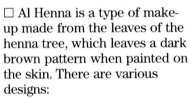

You could try this with face-paints, or buy henna from a chemist, but do not leave the mixture on your skin too long as it will stain.

EGYPT

♣ Try this recipe for Mashi kusa (stuffed courgettes)

Ingredients:
1 kg large courgettes
½ kg minced beef
4 onions, chopped
¼ kg rice
½ kg tomatoes
salt and pepper to taste

1. Cut off one end of the courgettes and remove the seeds with a knife. Be careful not to harm the walls of the courgettes. Sprinkle them lightly with salt and leave them for an hour.
2. Boil the rice according to the instructions on the packet.
3. Fry the onions and minced meat gently until it goes brown.
4. Stuff the courgettes with minced meat, onions, rice, salt and pepper and place in a well-greased baking tin.
4. Peel and cook the tomatoes and pour over the courgettes.
5. Cook in a moderate oven (Gas mark 5/375° F/190° C) for 1½ hours.

IDEAS FROM ALL OVER THE WORLD

☐ Choose three countries whose Promise, Law and Programme are very different from ours. What do you think about them?

♣ Hold an international fashion show with a sari, kimono, Ugandan traditional dress, Jamaican fold dress and some uniforms.

Don't forget what an important part music plays in all parts of the world. There are so many traditional folk dances, like the flamenco from Spain danced by the gypsies, or the dances of the Balinese which tell the stories of the Hindu gods, or Maori dances. Songs and musical instruments are often typical of the place where they originate – yodelling from Switzerland, the chants of Africa, the sitar from India, the gamelan from Indonesia and the Arabic ud.

☐ Try to borrow tapes of music from other lands and listen to them. Do you like the sounds? What do they make you think of?

INTERNATIONAL PEN-FRIENDS

A great way to find out about other Guides around the world is to have a pen-friend. If you write to the Post Box Secretary at one of these addresses she will put you in touch with someone. You should include:

Your name and address
Your date of birth Your choice of country, plus a second choice
Any languages you speak
The name of your Guide Company
A stamped, addressed envelope

ENGLAND
The International Department, The Girl Guides Association, 17–19 Buckingham Palace Road, London SW1W OPT

ULSTER
Ulster Girl Guide Headquarters, 38 Dublin Road, Belfast BT2 7HN

SCOTLAND
Scottish Girl Guide Headquarters, 16 Coates Crescent, Edinburgh EH3 7AH

WALES
Guides Cymru Office, Broneirion, Llandinam, Powys SY17 5DE

GOING ABROAD

You may get the chance to go abroad as a Guide, either with your own unit, or with a group made up from your own area. Or, if you are lucky, as a member of an official group representing the United Kingdom at an international event. There are also many international camps run in the UK you might attend. So keep your eyes open and grab any chance to meet and share with Guides and Girl Scouts at one of these events. When you're a Ranger these opportunities increase and you may even get the chance to live for a while with a family in another country, or take part in community projects.

When you travel abroad, you can take an International Introduction Card, which may help you to meet Guides and Girl Scouts from the country you are visiting. If you are with a Guide group, the leader will apply for this. If not, ask your Guider to get an application form for you

If you go on holidays abroad, look out for Guides and Girl Scouts in the countries you visit. Take some County or Country Badges with you for swaps.

LIVING ABROAD

If you go and live abroad you can take your Guiding with you! You can either join a unit of Guides or Girl Scouts of the country in which you are living or, if this is not practical because of language or other reasons, look for a British Guide unit nearby. If there is one it will probably be attached to the school. Units like this are part of British Guides in Foreign Countries and Guides in them use this handbook and follow the British Programme.

Whatever you do, remember to ask your home Guider for your record sheet and a transfer form, so your new Guider knows what you have done. A useful contact is your County Commonwealth and International Adviser (CCIA). You can ask her for any information about World Guiding you need to know.

And finally . . .

Remember what BP said: 'Look wide – and when you think you're looking wide, look wider!'

Guide Action is all about getting involved – not just walking by and letting someone else take the responsibility. Helping others, either on your own or as part of your Patrol, is an important part of Guiding and a really practical **throw** *way of showing commitment to your Promise.*

9

BE PREPARED

'I learnt it when I was a Guide', is often said by people coping with emergencies. Don't let your opportunity find you unprepared and useless. It might come tomorrow, so start preparing today.

Most of the activities in this chapter will help towards the Trefoil Badges.

Be prepared to help yourself. Could you:
- find a torch or candles if there was a power cut?
- open a jammed jar?
- make a call from a payphone?
- dress in the dark?
- find a spare light bulb and put it into the light fitting?
- stop the flow of hot and cold water?
- find and fit the correct fuse?
- undo a very tight knot?
- unjam a zip?
- know what to do if there was a gas leak?
- make a snack meal with what is in the store cupboard?

Be prepared to help your family. Could you:
- amuse a small child for half an hour?
- put on a car handbrake?
- pack a bag for someone who is going into hospital in a hurry?
- do the washing-up?
- mend a bicycle puncture?
- re-wire a plug?

Think of some other useful things you can do around the house and for others.

Be prepared to help others. Could you:
- help a blind person get on and off a bus?
- greet a visitor from another country?
- walk someone else's dog?
- put up a pushchair?
- make an emergency telephone call?
- notice and recognize a lost child?
- take a message accurately from one person to another?

- You might be asked for information – plan not to be caught out at any time. What might you be asked? Here are some ideas.

ROADS
Which roads near your home lead to the nearby towns and villages? How far are they?

SKETCH-MAPS
Learn to draw quick maps to explain directions to places in your home area.

LOCAL FACILITIES
Find your nearest:
Payphone and/or card phone
Post office
Doctor and/or hospital
Duty chemist
Petrol station
Police station
Places of worship

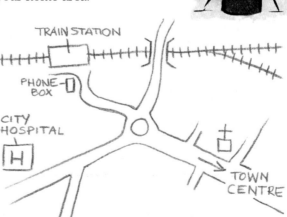

RECREATION

Would you know where to take a visitor to your area? Find out what they would enjoy – the leisure centre, a local museum, park or nature trail.

SERVICE

Guide Action is giving on-the-spot help when it is needed, but Guides help in other ways too. Often your Patrol or unit will be involved in a planned piece of service – something you are asked to do, or meeting a need someone in the unit has spotted.

There are often large-scale service projects organized by the GGA or your Country Region or another organization you could become involved in. Every piece of local service you do adds up to make a better world, but sometimes a service event for lots of people can really 'take off' and change people's attitudes – look at the way people have become more conservation-minded over the last few years!

Any project, whether large or small, needs planning and organizing if it is going to work.

You don't have to look very far to find something helpful to do. Here are some ideas of ways to help your family, neighbours, elderly or disabled people. All these suggestions are for things you can do alone.

☐ Do housekeeping tasks like vacuuming or washing windows.
☐ Rake leaves, weed gardens.
☐ Go on shopping or other errands.
☐ Become a Pack Leader with Brownies, or help with a Rainbow unit.
☐ Make banners or a poster for your place of worship.
☐ Amuse small children.
☐ Play cards with elderly people.
☐ Read to people with visual problems.
☐ Help to tidy up your local church garden or community centre.
☐ Ask an elderly person to share her knowledge of a subject or activity that interests you such as gardening, travel, history of Guiding and Scouting.

It's fun to do service projects together in a group or as a Patrol – the work gets shared so it gets done quicker! Below you'll find some ideas for things your Patrol can do, but the best ones come from exploring your own abilities and the needs of your community, so adopt and adapt!

PLANNING

First ask yourself:
– What am I good at?
– What are my interests?
– What are the needs of my community?
– How can I use my talents to help others?
– Who could help me do that?
– How much time can I give?

Don't start a long-term project if you won't have the time to keep it going – you may find that setting yourself a target and meeting it works better for you than something which may carry on for years.

In developing your plans, you'll have to ask one more important question:
– Will you need money for what you want to do?
If your answer is yes, how will you get it?

CARRYING IT OUT

Once you've made all your plans you can make a start. Be flexible: don't be discouraged if your plan has to be changed. Maybe someone who you thought would lend a hand can't do it – look for help from other people.

EVALUATION

When you are finished, get together and think about which parts worked and which parts didn't. This will help you with future projects.

Think about how you have kept your Promise through your service, not just in helping other people but in other ways too. Which of the Guide Laws have you been keeping?

How have you done your duty to God?

Have you served the Queen by serving the community?

Remember too that 'service' means doing things for no pay, and that you will be trusted to finish the job, and to do your best!

Here are some ideas for Patrol or group projects

☐ Do a survey on litter collection. Are there enough litter bins in your area? How can you encourage people to take more responsibility for their litter?

☐ Find out if there is an old person who would like a bird table. Make one and then put it up and keep it 'stocked'.

☐ Find out from the RSPB or a similar organization (see page 96 for addresses) about local projects (to put up nest-boxes, bat-boxes, owl-boxes and so on) and join in whatever they are doing.

☐ Get involved in local conservation work, such as clearing and replanting waste-ground, pond surveys and tree-planting.

☐ Find out about and help recycling projects. You could collect bottles from the housebound and take them to the bottlebank regularly. Or you could help with a local newspaper collection by collecting them from friends and neighbours or by helping to bundle and tie them together.

☐ Join in annual media appeals like the *Blue Peter* appeal, Comic Relief and 'Children in Need'.

☐ Help a service team maintain a local Scout or Guide camp site.

☐ Get involved in improving your area by planting and caring for hanging baskets and window boxes. Ask the local horticultural society, parks department or a gardener for help.

☐ Collect good used books and toys. Repair them if necessary and then give them to a crèche, hospital, children's home or other place where they will be of use.

☐ Find out if the local old people's club or home wants paperbacks for its members to read. If they do collect them and pass them on.

☐ Invite elderly people to be speakers and guests at Guiding activities.

☐ Ask a retired person to help with a service project you would like to do in your community.

☐ Find out about the projects run by Our Cabaña and Sangam, two of the World Centres. Can you publicize them and raise funds? Find out about special overseas and national projects supported by Guiding and help by raising funds for them. If anyone from your area is chosen to help abroad on one of these they could be invited to tell you about them. Ask your Guider to find out more from your County Commonwealth and International Adviser.

☐ Support the Girl Guide Friendship Fund. Or fund raise in your District for disaster relief appeal or a relief agency such as Save the Children Fund.

☐ Join a group making 'talking newspapers' for the visually handicapped.

☐ If you have visually handicapped friends, use your new skills to make tapes of *GUIDE PATROL* and your favourite magazines.

☐ Is your Guide meeting place accessible to people with disabilities? If not, how could it be improved? Can you make any changes?

☐ Ask a group from an organization such as PHAB (Physically Handicapped and Able Bodied) if they would like to share an evening with your Patrol or unit.

☐ Plan and organize a nature trail for Rainbows.

☐ Raise funds to send a Brownie on Pack Holiday.

☐ Help an adult run a 'lost child' centre or a crèche at a big local event.

☐ If you live by the sea or near mountains find out about the emergency services. Is there any way you can support what they do? Even if you do not live near the sea or mountains you can still support organisations such as the RNLI or the Mountain Rescue Team.

☐ For more ideas and guidelines on how to carry out community service projects, ask your Guider to obtain a copy of the GGA's 'Community Activity Pack'.

You sometimes need skills to be able to help others – that's part of being prepared. Would you like to learn a skill just to be able to be of help? Try one of these:

☐ Learn to use British Sign Language so that you can hold a conversation with someone who is deaf. Could you teach the signs to your Patrol?

☐ Learn how to plan and run games and activities for young children. Offer your help to others at birthday parties. Puppet and magic shows are fun to do. Help at District Brownie or Rainbow events.

PACK LEADER

If you have been a Guide for at least a year you may be asked to be a Pack Leader. This is an important job, for as well as helping at Brownie meetings, the Pack Leader's most important job is to be a link between the Pack and your Guide Company and to keep each informed about the other. Talk to your Guider if you feel you might like to give service in this way. It's also a good way to get a taste of leadership.

EMERGENCY ACTION

Our Founder, B-P said many years ago: 'Be prepared, that is, be ready for any kind of duty that may be thrust upon you, having practised it beforehand ... when others are perhaps dazed or flustered, you will come quietly forward and do the right thing.' One of the most important things that Guides do is learning how to cope in an emergency — knowing about first aid, safety at home and outside and how to improvise when there's a problem.

Guides also know that they can't do everything on their own — they know when to ask someone else to join in, because one person isn't always enough — however much you think you can cope, it's always best to work as a team with someone else.

FIRST AID

First aid is just that – on-the-spot help given to someone with an injury. Sometimes first aid won't be enough and medical help will be needed, but first aid can actually save lives. Lots of people have died just because the first people on the scene didn't know basic first aid – so Be Prepared by learning some simple techniques now!

BLEEDING
SMALL CUTS AND GRAZES

Clean the wound by holding it under running water or by wiping it with clean gauze. If the cut is still bleeding, hold it under running water until the bleeding stops.

Wipe away from the wound and use a new piece of gauze or wipe every time. (You can cut the wipe into smaller pieces with clean scissors.)

Cover the wound with a sticking plaster. If the wound is too large for a plaster, use a piece of dry dressing or gauze and sticky tape to make a protective cover. Use Micropore tape if the patient is allergic to ordinary sticking plaster.

MORE SERIOUS CUTS AND WOUNDS

Sometimes you will have to stop a wound bleeding before you can clean or dress it.

First raise the affected part of the body if possible – if a leg, make the patient lie down with her leg up, if an arm, make her sit down and hold her arm above her head.

Press firmly on the wound with a clean pad – a handkerchief, folded scarf or whatever you have handy. If blood soaks through the pad, don't take it away, just add another one and keep pressing on the wound until the bleeding stops. Keep the pad in place with a bandage, if you have one. Treat the patient for shock.

To treat really serious bleeding you can use this sort of direct pressure, but it's also a good idea to know something about **pressure points** – ask someone from the Red Cross, St John Ambulance or St Andrew's Ambulance Association to give your Patrol or unit information on more advanced first aid.

If there is anything stuck in the wound, like a piece of glass or wood, leave it there and seek medical help. Try to stop the bleeding by pressing above and below the wound. Raise the limb and gently lie a piece of gauze over the wound and build a 'wall' of cotton-wool pads around the object and as high as it. Don't push the object any deeper when you bandage it.

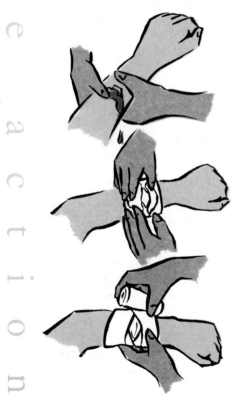

NOSEBLEEDS

Sit the casualty down.

Ask her to pinch the soft part of her nose.

Undo her collar.

She may have to hold her nose for ten minutes – ask her to spit into a bowl instead of swallowing.

Tell her not to blow her nose for a few hours, or the bleeding may start again.

If the bleeding doesn't stop, get medical help.

SCALDS AND BURNS

A **scald** happens when someone comes into contact with wet heat like boiling water, fat or steam.

A **burn** happens when someone touches something which is very hot – fire, a hot iron, or a lighted cigarette. Other types of burns are

– **friction burns** (like rope burns)

– **electrical burns**, which can happen if someone gets an electric shock

– **chemical burns**, which can happen if acid or corrosive liquid is spilt.

If someone gets a small scald or burn, you should cool the area as quickly as possible. The best way to do this is to hold it

under a running cold tap, or gently pour cold water over it. If you are at camp, and someone burns or scalds a hand or foot, hold the affected area in a bowl or bucket of cold water.

Keep the injury under the water for at least ten minutes or until the pain has stopped.

Gently remove rings, watches, shoes or anything else around the affected area before it begins to swell.

When the pain dies down, dry the area carefully (it will be very tender) and put on a clean (sterile if you have one) non-fluffy dressing such as Melonin or gauze. Fix the dressing in place with a bandage.

Any burn which is more than 2–3 cm across, or which is very painful even after it has been soaked in cold water, should be treated by a doctor or in hospital. Small children and elderly people should always have medical attention.

With burns and scalds:
● Never break blisters
● Never put on creams or lotions
● Never use sticking plaster
● Treat for shock

Treat a rope burn as a minor burn – cool it down and, if the skin is broken, clean it and cover with a small dressing.

MORE SERIOUS BURNS AND SCALDS

Your first aid should still be to cool the area as quickly as possible, but there are other things to think about as well:
● Send for adult or medical help, or get the casualty to hospital as soon as possible.
● (For a scald) Carefully remove any boiling wet clothing as it begins to cool – **do not** do this with a burn.
● Do not break blisters or touch loose skin.
● Treat for shock.

Chemical burns

These are very serious and you should not put yourself in any danger to apply first aid. Treat them as serious burns and get the casualty to hospital at once.

If you or someone else gets a splash of chemical in the eye,

you must wash it out with cold water as soon as possible.

Make sure the water runs straight away from the eye and not across the face.

Chemical burns can happen in various places:
– at home (bleaches, paint strippers, etc)
– at school (in the chemistry lab)
– outside (e.g. at a road accident).

Electrical burns

See Electric Shock on page 194.

Be Prepared to deal with emergencies:
● read the warning on the labels of household liquids
● read notices in the chemistry lab at school
● find out about Hazchems – the labels on tankers and lorries which give details of their contents
● don't put yourself at risk – another casualty is no good at all!

A much better idea is to make sure chemical burns can't happen at all:
● keep household poisons and liquids locked up or out of childrens' reach
● always wear the necessary safety equiment, e.g. gloves, goggles, when you use chemicals at home or at school.

FRACTURES

A casualty may be able to tell you she thinks she has broken a bone – she may have heard a crack, or she may not be able to walk or use her arm, or a limb may be the wrong shape or look twisted or odd.
Move her as little as possible.
Keep the limb still.
Send for an ambulance.
Treat her for shock.

FRACTURED SPINE

If a casualty has no feeling in her legs or arms, or says she feels shooting pains around her body, she may have a fractured spine. If you suspect this, it is important that you move her as little as possible, but send for an ambulance right away. Make her as comfortable as you can in the position you find her.

BRUISES

Soak a handkerchief or tea towel in cold water and wring it out. Make a pad of it (this is called a cold compress) and hold over the affected area. This helps to reduce swelling. Make the casualty comfortable.

SPRAINS

A sprained ankle or wrist may be so painful that it looks like a break, and the casualty may hardly be able to move the joint, if at all.

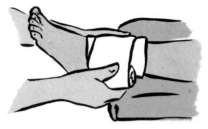

Rest the limb and raise it so it is comfortable.
Put on a cold compress to reduce swelling.
Support the injury with a firm dressing of cotton wool and a bandage.
Keep the limb raised and supported.

Cramp can be painful, but you can give first aid by stretching the affected muscles.

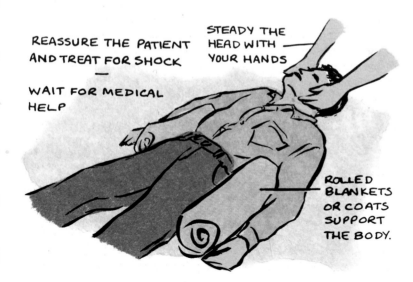

REASSURE THE PATIENT AND TREAT FOR SHOCK

WAIT FOR MEDICAL HELP

STEADY THE HEAD WITH YOUR HANDS

ROLLED BLANKETS OR COATS SUPPORT THE BODY.

STINGS

At camp a sharp sting is usually a sting from a wasp or another insect which should be treated with a cold compress. Remove a bee sting with tweezers, close to the skin so you don't squeeze the poison into the casualty, treat with a cold compress and rest.

SPLINTERS

Clean around the splinter with soap and water, then use sterilised tweezers to gently pull out the splinter.

If the splinter snaps, don't dig around in the wound but take the casualty to a doctor or to hospital, as she may need a tetanus injection.

To sterilise tweezers

(Let them cool down first!)

BLISTERS

You should never burst a blister over a burn – it's a sac of fluid protecting the tender skin beneath. However, sometimes a blister caused by something like a boot rubbing will hurt so much that it may be best to burst it carefully, using a needle sterilised in a match flame. Pierce at skin level in two places.
Press out the fluid with a clean piece of cotton wool.
Cover the blister with a sticking plaster.

CHOKING

If someone swallows something which 'goes the wrong way', she will cough and splutter and start to choke. If she is coughing, let her carry on, but if she can't, get her to bend over and slap her sharply between the shoulder blades four times. Sometimes she or you will have to use a finger to clear an obstruction from the mouth or throat.

POISONING

If you suspect that someone has eaten or drunk something poisonous, tell an adult and call a doctor or ambulance at once. The person who answers the phone may tell you how to help

before the doctor gets there.

Find out what the casualty has eaten or drunk – look for a bottle nearby and listen to what she is saying as you may have to tell the doctor.

If she becomes unconscious you may have to give her artificial ventilation (page 193). Take care you don't get any poison on you!

FAINTING

If someone feels faint she will feel dizzy, weak and may feel sick. Lie her down, lift her feet above the level of her heart and loosen any tight clothing. Keep a space around her and fan her face if necessary. She should feel better very quickly as the blood returns to her brain. If someone actually does faint, do the same thing. If there isn't space to lie her down, sit her with her head between her knees.

HYPOTHERMIA

Hypothermia is something which happens when the body temperature drops below normal, which is 36–37°C. It can happen if someone sits for a long time in an cold room, or if you get really wet through and stay wet for a long time, or if you don't wear clothes to keep you warm on a hike or at camp.

If you're out on a hike and one of the people you're with begins to drop behind, seems tired and slow, and starts to lose her temper, she may have hypothermia. Unless you are very close to where you are going, you should stop at once and shelter her as much as possible – wrap her in an emergency blanket or put up a tent around her. Lie her on a groundsheet or camping mat and send two of your party for help.

If she has any wet clothes on, take them off and put on dry ones, including a woolly hat. Give her a hot drink. If she becomes unconscious, put her in the recovery position, and keep checking her breathing.

The people who go for help should arrange for an ambulance or mountain rescue team to get her to hospital.

If everyone on the hike is dressed for warmth and keeps dry, no one should get hypothermia. However, you should always keep an eye on everyone in the group, as it can be very dangerous.

Hypothermia at home can happen to elderly people who don't like to heat their houses too much. If you find anyone at home with hypothermia symptoms, you should wrap them loosely in a blanket and put a woolly hat on them. Give them a warm drink such as milk or cocoa and get a doctor.

Never treat hypothermia by giving the casualty a hot water bottle, alcohol or by rubbing the skin or making them move around to 'warm up' – this will divert body heat from where it is most needed.

SUNBURN

It's so easy to become sunburnt, even when the sun doesn't seem very strong. If you're out in the sun you should wear a sunscreen cream and protect your head and neck with a hat or scarf.

If someone gets sunburnt, her skin will feel warm or hot to the touch and may be very red. Move her into the shade and give her plenty of water to drink. Mild sunburn can be eased with after-sun creams, but remember, prevention is better than cure!

ACCIDENTS

A first aider at an accident where someone is unconscious always starts with ABC:
**Airway
Breathing
Circulation**

(And if she can, she sends someone for medical help straightaway!)

A – Make sure the airway is clear by tilting the head back and lifting the lower jaw forward.

(If you suspect the casualty may have a fractured neck, don't move the head – just move the lower jaw forward.)

If the casualty isn't breathing when you find her, she might start straight away when you tilt her head back. Put your ear next to her mouth and watch for any movement of the chest. Look and listen carefully.

Check also that the airway isn't blocked by false teeth or vomit – if so, turn the head to

one side and clear the mouth using two fingers.

If she still isn't breathing, you need to use artificial ventilation.

B – to start breathing using artificial ventilation, first open and clear the airway as above. Keep the head back and the mouth open. Pinch the nostrils to close them. Keep the head in this position.

Take a deep breath and place your mouth over the casualty's mouth and blow gently into the casualty with enough force to make her chest rise.

Remove your mouth from the casualty and look along the chest – it should be falling as the air comes out.

Repeat the breath and check to see if her heart is beating. If it is, keep giving mouth-to-

mouth ventilation at a rate of once every four seconds.

When the casualty begins to breathe again, put her into the recovery position.

If the chest does not rise, at the first breath, check that you are holding the airway open properly.

If the casualty's mouth is injured, you might have to give mouth-to-

nose ventilation. Hold the mouth closed and seal your mouth over her nostrils.

Learn artificial ventilation from a qualified first aid instructor and always use a dummy – never a living person – to practise it.

C – If the casualty is not breathing and doesn't start, even after artificial ventilation, check the

circulation by finding a pulse.

If there is no pulse, the heart has stopped and someone must restart it with external

chest compression at once. External chest compression is a vital first aid technique, but it is one you should learn from a qualified instructor and never practise on a living person, as it can sometimes cause a lot of harm. Why not ask your Guider or Patrol Leaders' Council to ask an expert to teach you first aid at your meeting?

TREATING SOMEONE FOR SHOCK

If someone is injured she will probably be panicky and frightened, which you would expect, but her body will also be upset and react in a way which is called **shock**. What happens is that the body sends blood to the heart, brain and other important internal organs, which means there is less blood available for the outside of the body. So a person with shock will:

- have pale or even grey, cold skin, sometimes sweaty
- feel weak, faint or dizzy
- breathe quickly, yawn or gasp
- have a weak, rapid pulse.

They may also:

- be thirsty
- feel sick (may even be sick)
- become unconscious.

Some people wear 'Medic-Alert' discs to tell first aiders and doctors of medical conditions they have – look for one of these around the neck or wrist.

The first aider's job is to stop the state of shock becoming so bad that the casualty becomes unconscious.

Lie the patient down with head to one side.

Talk to the patient all the time, reassuring her, telling her what you are doing, explaining that help is on its way.

Prop her legs up (unless she has a broken leg).

Loosen tight clothing.

Treat any obvious injuries.

Keep her warm.

Send for medical help.

Notice whether her breathing rate changes, and if she feels as if she will be sick or finds it difficult to breathe, or becomes unconscious, put her into the recovery position. Stay with her and keep reassuring her.

Electric Shock

Stop the electrical current by unplugging the equipment or turning off the electricity at the mains. Do not touch the casualty. Remember metal and water conduct electricity, wood, paper and rubber do not. Phone the hospital immediately.

THE RECOVERY POSITION

Used when someone is found or becomes unconscious, and especially if you have to leave a casualty to go for help.

**Kneel down.
Turn head up and
towards you.
Arms by sides, near
hand tucked under.
Move far arm
across chest.
Cross far leg over
near leg.**

**Support head with your
hand. Grasp clothing at hip
and lift body towards
you. Rest body
against your legs.
Keep airway open
by tilting head.
Bend arm and leg for support.**

**Move other arm out carefully.
Check airway is still open.
Make sure casualty cannot
roll forwards or back.
No more than half of chest
in contact with ground.**

The recovery position is used:
– to keep the airway open
– because if the casualty is sick
it will drain away and not choke
her.

Sometimes you won't be able to
use it if the casualty has a
broken limb, or if her spine may
be fractured. In this case, make
sure the airway is open (move
the casualty's head as little as
you have to) and support a
broken limb with a rolled-up
blanket or cushion.

IMPROVISATION

Bandages are used to support
injured limbs, or to hold a
dressing on a wound. Learn
how to do these:

Your Guide scarf can be used as an emergency triangular bandage in several ways. How often do you wash it?

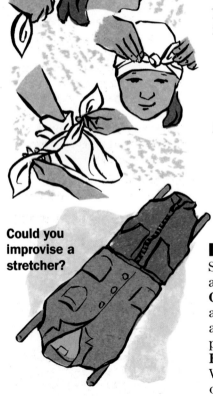

Could you improvise a stretcher?

Be prepared for accidents – make your own first aid kit!

CREPE BANDAGE

ABSORBANT COTTON

TRIANGULAR CALICO BANDAGE

SCISSORS

CONFORMING BANDAGE WITH CLIP

GAUZE BANDAGE

RUBBER GLOVES

PLASTERS

TWEEZERS

GAUZE BANDAGE

SAFETY PINS

STERILE DRESSING

IMITATION WOUNDS

Set up first aid incidents for another Patrol to treat.

Grazes: rub in a little Vaseline, add red poster paint or lipstick and then a little earth and a few pieces of gravel.

Burns: grease skin with Vaseline and redden with rouge or lipstick. Drop candle-grease 'blisters' on to a knife and, when cool, transfer to 'burn'.

Cuts: grease skin then put flat piece of flesh-coloured Plasticine in place and smooth edges into skin, cut into Plasticine with blunt edge and add 'blood'.

Face: powder with talcum or flour to make pale; rouge for a hectic flush.

Lips: pale shades, or dark brown lipsticks, or blue eye-shadows can be used to alter normal lip colour.

Experiment for yourselves with good 'blood' mixtures, 'broken' bones, or other realistic ideas.

Make your 'incidents' as real as possible, so that it is a practice in assessing what has happened and what should be done. Use your good actresses as casualties until everyone learns how to behave in a realistic way. People who just giggle are no use.

ANY KIND OF EMERGENCY
Gas leak
Heart attack
Robbery
Accident
Someone fallen in the canal
Fire at home

Could you cope?

Here are some activities for you to try:
☐ Having a list of emergency numbers ready in advance can be a life-saver. Make a list of emergency numbers such as your mum's and dad's work numbers, neighbours, doctor, dentist, local police station and main services e.g. gas, water, electric. Put a copy next to the telephone in your home. Keep the list up-to-date and add other telephone numbers as you think of them.

☐ Practise making emergency phone calls with a friend using a toy phone or a disconnected one (whatever you do don't make a real call). Learn how to give the most important information quickly and how to follow directions given to you.

☐ Practise remembering messages. Ask your Guider to give you a message at the beginning of a meeting. Try repeating it half an hour later.

☐ Practise memorizing details like car numbers, people's descriptions and so on so that you are able to clearly describe things that have happened.

☐ Practise describing scenes remembering what you see, smell and hear.

☐ Play observation games to improve your memory. Ask your Guider to prepare a tray with 20 different objects on it. Look at them for one minute, remove the tray and try to write down all the objects.

☐ Ask the local police to come and tell you how they use information from witnesses in their work.

☐ Find out where the following are in your home, if you have them:

– the fuse box
– the mains water tap
– the mains gas tap
– the boiler or hot water heater
– the thermostat.

Find out emergency procedures for at least one of them, for example, how to shut the water off.

☐ Look through your home for things that might be poisonous, such as medicines, cleaning fluids, and weed-killers. Make sure they are labelled and stored in a safe place, out of the reach of young children.

☐ Invite a first aider to your meeting with a 'Resusci-Annie' to learn and practise mouth-to-mouth ventilation and external chest compression.

Learn how to use a rope to rescue someone from a river:

You will find these knots useful

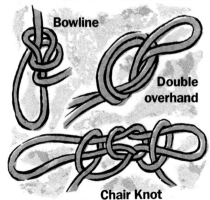

Bowline

Double overhand

Chair Knot

Carrying a casualty

FIRE SAFETY

Most fires happen because people are careless. It is easier to prevent fires than fight them.

What are the fire hazards in this picture?

☐ Have a fire prevention campaign. Check your home to see if it has any fire hazards. If you haven't got them already, suggest to your family that they install smoke alarms – more people are killed by fumes than fire, so early warning is vital.

☐ Look at your meeting place for fire hazards. If you find any, suggest to the owners that something is done about them.

Work out a fire drill for your house and/or meeting place. How would you manage if there were people in wheelchairs or pushchairs with you? Hold a fire drill and see how long it would take to clear the building.

HOME FIRE DRILL

If you suspect a fire:

1. Alert everyone in the house. Shout 'Fire!' and get them out of the house as quickly as you can. Don't stop to get dressed or collect anything – just grab a coat or blanket and go!

2. As you leave the house, close all doors. An ordinary house door can hold a fire back for 30 minutes.

3. Dial 999 at a neighbour's house or a call box and ask for the Fire Service. Give your name and address clearly and explain where you are.

4. Do not go back into the house – no possession or pet is worth the risk.

Don't waste time fighting the fire. Get out and get help as quickly as you can.

If you get trapped in a burning building:

1. Close the door and block the gap under it with a rug or coat.

2. Get out of the window if you are on the ground floor, or go to the window and attract attention by shouting and waving.

3. If you have to get out of an upstairs window, don't jump – throw out blankets, cushions, etc to break your fall, then lower yourself from the sill and drop gently. Roll over on landing. (You will only be able to do this if there are no flames below you. The best policy is to wait by the window until the fire brigade arrive and get you out.)

If you become trapped in smoke, get down to floor level and make a mask out of a handkerchief. Crawl to the nearest exit. Hot air, smoke and gases rise; the air will be fresher and cooler at floor level.

Whenever you visit a building for the first time always take note of where the fire exits are and the quickest routes to them. Do you know the fire escapes from your school? The supermarket? The sports centre?

Fire extinguishers:

If someone's clothing catches fire:

1. Lie the casualty down and smother the flames (cut off their oxygen supply) with water or a blanket or coat (made from natural materials – some synthetics can melt).

2. When the flames are out, treat for shock and give first aid for the burns. Call an ambulance and don't remove burnt clothing – it can help to keep the wound sterile.

BLACK FIRE EXTINGUISHERS ARE USUALLY FOR FIRES CAUSED BY AN ELECTRICAL FAULT.

o

RED FIRE EXTINGUISHERS ARE USUALLY FOR FIRES CAUSED BY PAPER, WOOD, CLOTH, ETC.

o

FOLLOW INSTRUCTIONS ON THE FIRE EXTINGUISHER CAREFULLY.

Chip pan fire

1. Turn off the heat under the pan.

2. Put on the pan lid or a damp tea towel. This cuts off the oxygen supply.

3. Leave to cool – do not take the lid off or the fire could start again.

Some people have a fire blanket in the kitchen for fires like this – if you have one make sure you know how to use it.

Never use water on a chip or frying pan fire – it will make the burning fat splash all over the place.

Never pick up a burning pan – deal with it on the stove.

WATER SAFETY – SIMPLE RULES TO KEEP YOU SAFE

'I'm all right – I can swim!' That's what you may think, but hundreds of people drown every year, and many of them thought that they would be all right becasue they could swim. Water is necessary for life but it can be treacherous, too – currents and cold can overcome even the strongest swimmers.

People can drown in the bath, in the sea, in canals, in swimming pools. They can fall into water unexpectedly when out walking or playing – in fact many people drown who weren't even 'out swimming' but fell into a canal or river by mistake.

How can you make sure that you and your family and friends stay safe in and near water?

In the swimming pool

– always check the depth at each end and in the middle
– never run
– stay within your depth unless you can swim well
– make sure there is a space before you dive or jump in
– do as you are told by the lifeguards.

Some pools have flumes, wave machines and waterchutes, which are great fun if you use them safely. Follow the pool rules. If you are swimming with your unit, stay with a group and don't go off on your own.

By the seaside

– only swim between the flags and never swim if the red flag is flying
– stay with other people
– swim along the shore, not away from it
– don't stay in too long; it's colder than you think!
– signal for help if you get into difficulties

– keep inflatable dinghies on a line attached to the shore
– never play on inflatable mattresses; you can drift out to sea too easily
– watch for changes in the weather, tide or currents and leave the water if everyone else does
– don't swim where people are water skiing, boardsailing or boating; they're moving too fast to stop for you!

By rivers, lakes and canals

– don't stand on overhanging banks

– don't walk too near to the edge of the water; one slip and you're under

– notice where lifebelts are positioned, just in case

– don't walk on frozen ponds no matter how thick the ice is; it may break under your weight

– don't let younger brothers and sisters play alone near garden ponds or paddling pools

– don't swim unless you know the water is safe for swimming and you have a lifeguard there. Set boundaries and keep to them. Many rivers, lakes and canals are polluted, so it's probably best not to swim in them.

Most of the time you won't be swimming in rivers, lakes or canals unless you have fallen out of a canoe or from a sailboard! If you do fall in, try not to drink the water and wash or shower afterwards.

WEIL'S DISEASE

Many stretches of water have a bacterium in them which can make you ill. If you have a cut or scratch you should cover it with a waterproof plaster before you go on the water. If you fall ill with flu-like symptoms within three weeks of a water activity, you should tell your doctor you have been canoeing (or whatever) and ask for a special blood test for Weil's Disease. It doesn't happen very often but it can make you very ill, so it's best to be safe.

WATER RESCUE

If you see someone in trouble in the water, don't jump to the rescue – you can drown yourself that way. Stay calm and:

● **Shout** for help if there are people nearby, or send someone for help if you are in a group.

● **Reach** using an umbrella, branch, pole or oar to the drowning person; or take off your jacket or jumper, wet it and reach with that. Shout and tell the person what you are doing. Lie on the bank so that you don't fall in yourself.

● **Throw** a rope or lifebelt, if there is one handy, then pull the person to the bank. Look around for anything that will float, such as a plastic bottle,

r–e–a–c–h

and throw it in front of the person so it doesn't land behind or even on her. Tell her to hold it to her chest and to kick her legs to the bank. Help her out of the water, taking care not to be pulled in.

If you are on your own and cannot reach or throw anything run as quickly as you can for help.

● **Wade** gradually, testing the depth of the water with a branch or pole, and reach towards the person as above. Don't wade unless you can secure yourself to the bank with a rope or by someone else holding you. Don't try to swim.

● **Row** – if there's a boat nearby and you know how to use it! Don't try to get the person into the boat, but tow her back to the bank.

Only if you're a qualified lifesaver should you try to rescue someone by swimming, and even then only when the 'Reach-Throw-Wade-Row' techniques don't work.

☐ Practise throwing a rope so that it reaches a target.
☐ Improvise possible water accidents with your Patrol. Give the drowning person clear, concise instructions explaining what you are doing.

10

the trefoils

Most Guides who join when they are ten

will start on the Yellow Trefoil

when they make their Promise.

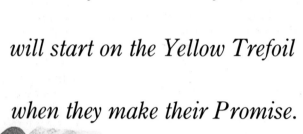

However, if you join Guides when you

are older than ten, you don't have to start at the

beginning – talk with your Guider about the best Trefoil for

you to start on. Each Trefoil

may take between nine and eighteen

months, so if you are in Guides for four to five years you

will be able to progress through them all.

YELLOW TREFOIL

I made my Promise on

. . . .

For the Yellow Trefoil you should show that you are trying to keep your Promise through doing the following:

1. Take part in at least six activities with your Patrol to gain new experiences in each of the Eight Points. (Remember, many activities cover more than one point.)

2. Decide on an activity you like doing. Show that you have made progress in it since starting your Yellow Trefoil. You could choose a hobby, a sport, a skill or a general interest and work towards an Interest Badge, a Patrol Interest Pennant or a similar award.

3. Choose one thing from each of these areas and show that you have done your best while working on each activity.

A1. Make something using a craft from another country.

2. Design something to wear for a special occasion.

3. Write a short play and act it out with your Patrol.

B1. Take part in an event with girls from one or more other unit/s and try to get to know them better.

2. With your Patrol, take part in an activity or game which helps you to learn about WAGGGS and/or the World Flag.

3. Find out about life in your community 50 years ago by talking to an older person.

C1. Know how to contact the Emergency Services. Make a list of emergency telephone numbers which your family might need and put them in a sensible place at home.

2. Learn how to treat someone for shock and how to put them in the recovery position. Find out what you can do at home to avoid accidents with gas, electricity, oil heaters and coal fires.

3. Take part in a Patrol service project.

D1. Find out how to wire a plug and change a fuse. Show someone else that you know how to do these things correctly.

2. Prepare and serve a simple meal. Make it look as appetizing as you can.

3. Find out how to remove stains from clothing and what the fabric-care symbols mean. Wash and iron a simple garment following the instructions on the label.

E1. Find out why exercise and healthy eating are important. Design and make 'healthy living' posters showing people of your own age what you have learnt.

2. Find out about food values. Make a chart showing your Patrol's favourite foods and see how healthy your diets are.

3. Take up an active sport or get better at one you already take part in.

F1. Make it your job to keep your Patrol/unit equipment tidy for a month.

2. Take up a new hobby and tell your Patrol how you are progressing with it after at least three months.

3. Find out about an endangered species, and what is being done to protect it. Tell your Patrol about it.

G1. Set and follow a trail.

2. With your Patrol, pitch a

tent.

3. Study an area of about 500 square metres near your home or meeting place and find out what plants, insects, animals and birds live in and use the area.

H1. Help your Patrol to work out and use a secret code.

2. Learn how to tie the following: reef knot, clove hitch, sheetbend, figure-of-eight knot, and round turn and two half-hitches. Find out how they are used.

3. Read an interesting book and tell your Patrol about it.

4. Meet a challenge which you have set yourself with help from your Guider and Patrol Leader.

5. Discuss with your Guider the reasons for choosing the things you have done for this Trefoil and what you have most enjoyed doing. Talk about how working for the Yellow Trefoil has helped you to make progress in Guiding and how it has helped you keep your Promise.

Yellow Trefoil gained

signed . . . .

date . . . .

GREEN TREFOIL

I made/ renewed my Promise on

. . . .

For your Green Trefoil you need to show you are trying to keep your Promise through doing the following:

1. Take a full part in your Patrol's activities to gain new experiences in each of the Eight Points. If possible try to take on a responsible job in some of these activities.

2. Work towards at least two badges and show how this has extended

your skills. (You could choose the Patrol Purpose Patch, the Patrol Interest Pennant, an Interest Badge taken as a Patrol, a Service Badge or a Religious Knowledge Badge.)

3. Choose one thing from each of these areas and show that you have done your best while working on each activity.

A1. Make puppets and put on a show with your Patrol.

2. Write a song telling how Guiding began and teach it to your Patrol.

3. Learn how to make your own stencils and create a design using them.

B1. Make a game about World Guiding and play it with your Patrol.

2. Learn about the difficulties faced by disabled people by trying some Cap-Handi activities with your Patrol.

3. Correspond with a pen-pal for at least three months and find out about his/her daily life.

C1. Make a pocket first-aid kit and know how to use it. Learn how to give artificial ventilation.

2. Learn how to simulate wounds and show how to treat them, including appropriate bandaging for sprains and breaks.

3. With your Patrol plan and carry out a service project such as raising funds for a charity, helping regularly at your place of worship or involvement in local conservation work.

D1. Make a simple toy or household article using wood, plastic or a similar material. Know how to use tools such as saws, hammers, screwdrivers, files and scissors correctly.

2. Cook a traditional dish from another country and share it with others.

3. Grow your own houseplant from seed or cuttings and look after it for at least three months.

E1. Plan a daily fitness routine and carry it out for at least one month.

2. Find out about the dangers of over-eating and over-dieting. Keep a diary of everything you eat for seven days and discuss it with an interested adult.

3. Learn a dance and teach it to your Patrol.

F1. Make an emergency sewing kit and show that you can do running repairs such as darning a hole, and mending a tear.

2. Try rewriting the Guide Law without using words like 'loyal', 'obedient', 'polite' and so on.

3. With your Patrol, visit the local shops and compare the prices of environmentally friendly products with the other ones. Make a poster to advertise them.

G1. Light a fire and cook a simple meal using it.

2. Learn how to use Ordnance Survey maps including scale, symbols and contour lines. With your Patrol explore an area using a map.

3. Make a rain gauge and use it to help you to keep a weather chart for at least a month.

H1. Learn how to keep simple accounts and use what you have learnt to help your Patrol, or to budget your pocket money.

2. Show how to set up, load and run some software on a computer, such as a game or drawing package.

3. Write an account of a Guide event for the local paper or your Patrol/unit log book.

4. Meet a challenge which you have set yourself with help from your Guider and Patrol Leader.

5. Discuss with your Guider the reasons for choosing the things you have done for this Trefoil and what you have most enjoyed doing. Talk about how working for the Green Trefoil has helped you to make progress in Guiding and how it has helped you keep your Promise.

Green Trefoil gained

signed . . . .

date . . . .

RED TREFOIL

I made/ renewed my Promise on

. . . .

For the Red Trefoil you need to show that you are trying to keep your Promise through doing the following:

1. Take responsibility in your Patrol and organize some of the activities you choose to do. Introduce something new to your Patrol or unit. (You can get ideas from the Patrol Interest Packs, Guider's PACs, *GUIDE PATROL* and other publications.)

2. Continue to extend your skills and knowledge by choosing at least one area of the Eight Point Programme and working towards a Collective Emblem, a Patrol Interest Pennant or the Guide Camp Permit.

3. Choose one thing from each of these areas and show that you have done your best while working on each activity.

the trefoils

A1. Try a traditional craft such as spinning, weaving, tatting, quilting or candle-making.

2. Use photographs and captions to tell a story.

3. With the help of colour charts, magazines or samples show how you would decorate and furnish your ideal room.

B1. With other Guides and/or Guiders visit a meeting of another youth organization. Find out what they do and whether they work for badges and, if so, what. Tell your Patrol/unit about your visit.

2. With your Patrol survey your meeting place or school(s) to find what adaptations have been made (or could be made) to help disabled people. Report on what you find.

3. With your Patrol plan and carry out an international activity.

C1. Be able to identify poisonous plants and berries which are found in your area, and know what to do if someone eats them, or swallows any other poisonous substances.

2. Design a fire prevention poster and know what to do if fire breaks out at home. Work out a fire drill for your meeting place and try it out.

3. Take on a regular commitment to help other people in some way for at least three months.

D1. Learn how to mend a puncture in a bicycle tyre or how to change a car wheel, and know how to carry out simple car maintenance such as checking the oil.

2. Make jam, pickles or other preserves.

3. Show that you can clean and look after the following: cooker, fridge, freezer, vacuum cleaner and sink unit.

E1. Find out about the harmful effects on health of alcohol, drugs, solvents and smoking, and discuss them with an adult.

2. Plan healthy menus for your family or a Guide event for at least two days. Try them out.

3. Have a go at exercises such as those used for relaxation. Use them for a month. See if they work for you.

F1. Make a collection of newspaper and magazine cuttings about people who show courage. Discuss your collection with your Patrol.

2. Make a game to teach to a new Guide what the Guide Law means.

3. Make a nest-box or a bat-box (or something similar) and put it in a suitable place.

G1. Learn how to use a Silva-type (protractor) compass and take part in an activity to show you can put what you have learnt into practise.

2. Take part in an incident hike with your Patrol using outdoor and camping skills.

3. Make and use a camp oven.

H1. Design and make a clock, a bridge or something similar.

2. Find out what route cards are and how to make them.

3. Write a review of a film, video, TV programme or record suitable for a teenage magazine.

4. Meet a challenge which you have set yourself with help from your Guider and Patrol Leader.

5. Discuss with your Guider the reasons for choosing the things you have done for this Trefoil and what you have most enjoyed doing. Talk about how working for the Red Trefoil has helped you to make progress in Guiding and how it has helped you keep your Promise.

Red Trefoil gained

signed . . . .

date . . . .

BLUE TREFOIL

I renewed my Promise on

. . . .

Before starting to work on the Blue Trefoil you must be thirteen-years-old and already hold at least one other Trefoil.

For the Blue Trefoil you need to show that you are trying to keep your Promise through doing the following:

1. Continue to take a full part in your Patrol activities and use what you have learnt so far to help your Patrol to undertake one of the following – a Patrol Purpose Patch, an Interest Badge as a Patrol, a Patrol Interest Pennant or a similar Patrol project.

2. Gain/use the Guide Camp Permit or gain a Collective Emblem.

3. Choose one thing from each of these areas and show that you have done your best while working on each activity.

A1. With your Patrol put on a musical evening which shows the skills of the whole Patrol. Include different types of music.

2. Using a craft which is new to you, make a small gift suitable for an elderly person.

3. Write a story or poem telling a local legend or custom to a visitor. Present it in an attractive way.

B1. Find out about the roles of girls and women in the different cultures represented in your area. Discuss what you discover with an interested adult.

2. Find out who your local councillor is, and invite him/her to your meeting to tell you about his/her job.

3. With the help of your Patrol, plan and hold an international evening.

C1. Know about and describe survival techniques and treatment for hypothermia and heat exhaustion.

2. Find out what materials can be recycled, and what recycling facilities there are in your area. Advertise the need for recycling, and help to organize the collection and disposal of recyclable materials.

3. Design and make a useful gadget or equivalent which would help a disabled person.

D1. Learn how to turn off gas (if available), electricity and water and demonstrate that you can stop a tap dripping. Read a gas and electricity meter.

2. Plan, prepare and serve in an attractive way a two-course meal including food which has not been processed before you buy it.

3. Make an article of clothing for yourself which shows you can work from a pattern and that you understand the importance of matching garment style to fabrics and yarns.

E1. Invite an expert to tell you about the problems caused by drug abuse in your area, and the precautions you can take to avoid the dangers.

2. Find out about the dietary needs of people with such conditions as diabetes, coeliac disease or high cholesterol levels. Survey the local shops to see where they can buy their food, and what it costs.

3. Try an adventurous activity such as climbing, canoeing, caving with the help of an expert.

F1. Organize a visit for your Patrol to a local firm to study how they are trying to protect the environment.

2. Think of six or more situations in which you have found it difficult to be loyal to family, friends and Guides. Discuss with an adult the problems caused by divided loyalties in life.

3. Survey the local banks and building societies and decide which offers the best package for you. Find out how to open an account there.

G1. With at least three others plan and go for a worthwhile expedition of at least 10 kilometres.

2. With your Patrol construct and use a rope bridge, raft or equivalent.

3. Learn about the common constellations and take part in a navigation exercise using the stars to guide you.

H1. Organize a wide game for one or two Patrols which will take at least 20 minutes to complete. (Your Guider must know your plans before you play the game.)

2. Discover what laws control part-time working in your area for someone your age. Find out what is available, and write a sample letter applying for a job.

3. Find out what the Electoral Roll is – where it can be seen and how and when you get your name onto it.

4. Find out as much as you can about Rangers and/or Young Leaders. Visit a Ranger Unit or Young Leader meeting or event. Tell your Patrol what you find out.

5. Discuss with your Guider the reasons for choosing the things you have done for this Trefoil and what you have most enjoyed doing. Talk about how working for the Blue Trefoil has helped you keep your Promise and how it has prepared you for the future.

Blue Trefoil gained

signed . . . .

date . . . .

THE BADEN-POWELL TREFOIL AWARD

You may start work for the Baden-Powell Trefoil any time after your thirteenth birthday and work for it at the same time as your Blue Trefoil, but you must finish the Blue Trefoil before the Baden-Powell Trefoil can be awarded.

1. On a suitable occasion agreed with your Guider, present in an interesting way all you can about one aspect of the history of Guiding, for example the development of the World Centres, the lives of Lord and Lady Baden-Powell or any four decades of Guiding.

2. Hold the Service Emblem and the Service Flash and show that you are continuing to be of service in the community.

3. Show that you are making progress in a hobby or craft, either by gaining an Interest Badge related to it, or by gaining a qualification from an outside body such as the Associated Board of the Royal School of Music, or by teaching your Patrol how to do it.

4. Take an active part in a Guide camp or an equivalent residential event for Guides while you are working for the Baden-Powell Trefoil.

5. Find out what is meant by the following terms: the EC, the Commonwealth, WAGGGS and explain these clearly to an interested adult. Hold the Commonwealth Badge, World Association Badge or Europe Badge.

6. Gain one of the following badges: Carpenter, Computer, Handywoman, or a badge involving homecraft skills.

Badges which are taken for the Baden-Powell Trefoil may not be used for the Blue Trefoil

When you have finished the Baden-Powell Trefoil arrange a visit to your District Commissioner and take with you your completed Baden-Powell Trefoil record. Talk with her about how you feel your understanding of the Promise has grown while you have been in your Guide Company and how your Promise will help you in the future.

the trefoils

PS

Times change ... and so do Guides! It's easy, when you've been in Guides for a while, to feel you've done it all.

You might want to try new things,

to be responsible for yourself a bit more

and (occasionally) to get away from

having to help the younger ones!

Or you might want to help

with Rainbows, Brownies or Guides.

You may have come to the end of your Guide Handbook, but you certainly needn't think you have come to the end of Guiding! There's lots more for you — in fact, a great wide world to explore and enjoy! But, before you begin to consider what will be your next steps in Guiding, take a few minutes to think about and judge for yourself what being a Guide has meant for you in terms of learning and growing, of making friends, and of developing a set of values to help you live your life to the full.

Looking back on all the activities you have done as a Guide decide what has been:

☐ **something which went well from start to finish**

☐ **something which went disastrously wrong**

☐ **your biggest challenge**

☐ **your most unforgettable moment**

☐ **your most frightening moment**

☐ **the moment when you almost gave up**

☐ **the best contribution you ever made to your Patrol**

☐ **the greatest fun.**

SO, WHAT NEXT?

When you are 13, you can start on ACTION PLUS!

ACTION PLUS is something extra for older Guides and other girls your age. It's a way of doing all the things you most like in Guiding – and trying new activities as well!

ACTION PLUS has activities and ideas in four areas: Adventure, Community, Creativity, Wider World. You can count ACTION PLUS activities towards the Trefoils or you can join in if you are slow getting through Trefoils and just want to extend your Guiding fun. You can do the activities in the ACTION PLUS programme by yourself or with others. Find out more – get hold of the ACTION PLUS book. Your Guider should have a copy or it's available from the GGA Trading Service and Guide shops.

When you are 14 you can start on the Duke of Edinburgh's Award Scheme and incorporate it into your Guiding. There are three stages: Bronze for people over 14, Silver for people over 15 and Gold for people over 16.

If you start on the Award Scheme at school, talk to your supervisor about how you can make some of your Guiding activities count towards Duke of Edinburgh and vice versa. In every Guide County there should be an Adviser for the Duke of Edinburgh's Award Scheme to help you plan your activities so that you don't end up doing everything twice! Your Guider or Commissioner will be able to give her name and address for you to contact her.

Then there is the senior section of Guiding – for young women who have finished being Guides but want to move on to enjoy a new and challenging action-packed programme designed especially for them. And there is a special opportunity waiting for you if you feel you want to stay in the Movement to become a leader working with Rainbows, Brownies and Guides. You will be able to receive the right sort of practical training which will enable you to gain leadership skills for Guiding, and for life.

Before you decide talk to your Guider! Tell her what you have enjoyed, where you are going next and what you want to do. And whether you stay in Guiding forever or decide to take a break, keep in touch! **GOOD LUCK!**

Caroline Smith

GUIDE PATROL

the only magazine specially designed to assist with *all* your Guide activities.

It's fresh, fun and full of fascinating facts. So if you're keen to try something new, hooked on good Guiding or simply stuck for ideas *GUIDE PATROL* can help.

To get this essential aid to great Guiding every month just place a regular order with your local newsagent or take out a subscription from CHQ.

Hit target every time with *GUIDE PATROL.*

To:
Magazine Subscriptions Department,
The Girl Guides Association,
17-19 Buckingham Palace Road,
LONDON,
SW1W 0PT.

Please send me a subscription form for *GUIDE PATROL*
magazine.

Name_____

Address_____

_____

Post Code_____

Signed_____

Date_____